INTRODUCING
THE
NEW TESTAMENT

INTRODUCING
THE
NEW TESTAMENT

by

Archibald M. Hunter

SECOND EDITION
REVISED AND ENLARGED

Philadelphia
THE WESTMINSTER PRESS

First published in Great Britain
by the S. C. M. Press, Ltd.

FIRST EDITION, 1945
SECOND EDITION, *Revised and Enlarged, 1957*

Library of Congress Catalog Card No.: 58–5256

Typeset in Great Britain
Printed in the United States of America

CONTENTS

PAGE

Preface   7

Part One: INTRODUCTORY

I   Why We Study the New Testament   9
II   Language, Text and Canon   17
III   The Contents of the New Testament   26

Part Two: THE FOUR GOSPELS

IV   How the Gospels came to be Written   29
V   The Synoptic Problem: A Literary
      Puzzle   34
VI   The Earliest Gospel (Mark)   40
VII   The Gentile Christian Gospel (Luke) 48
VIII The Jewish Christian Gospel (Matthew) 55
IX   The Spiritual Gospel (John)   61

Part Three: THE EARLY CHURCH AND ST PAUL

X   How They Brought the Good News from
      Jerusalem to Rome (Acts)   70
XI   St Paul   79
XII   The Gospel According to St Paul
      (Romans)   91
XIII The Church of God in Vanity Fair
      (I Corinthians)   97
XIV   The Trials and Triumphs of an Apostle
      (II Corinthians)   105
XV   Christian Freedom (Galatians)   112
XVI   The Glory of the Church (Ephesians) 120

Contents

PAGE

XVII   A Paean from Prison (Philippians)   128

XVIII   The Cosmic Christ (Colossians)   134

XIX   Saints in Salonica (I and II Thessalonians)   139

XX   Speaking the Truth in Love (Philemon)   143

XXI   The Pastoral Epistles (I and II Timothy and Titus)   148

Part Four: THE WRITINGS OF THE OTHER APOSTOLIC MEN

XXII   The Epistle of Priesthood (Hebrews)   157

XXIII   The Epistle of Practice (James)   164

XXIV   The Epistle of Hope (I Peter)   168

XXV   The Correspondence of the Elder (I, II and III John)   174

XXVI   Contending for the Faith (Jude)   182

XXVII   The Promise of His Coming (II Peter)   184

XXVIII   The Judgment and Victory of God (Revelation)   186

Epilogue: THE UNITY OF THE NEW TESTAMENT   195

Bibliography   201

Indexes   205

PREFACE

WHEN I wrote this little Introduction in 1945, I sought to mediate the findings of the New Testament scholars in a simple untechnical form. Many, I am grateful to say, found the book useful. But these were austere days in 1945, and, because I was limited to 40,000 words, I must needs confine myself to what I deemed the more important among the New Testament's twenty-seven books. Now, however, the SCM Press have allowed me to fill in the gaps—the new chapters are 14, 15, 16, 18, 19, 21, 25, 26 and 27—and I hope that in this 'definitive' form (if so pretentious an adjective may be applied to so small a book) it will serve its original purpose even better.

A. M. HUNTER

Aberdeen University
1957

PART ONE

INTRODUCTORY

I

Why We Study the New Testament

IF an unbeliever, or some seeker after God, were to ask us, 'Why should I study the New Testament? What is there in this book to be found in no other?' how should we answer?

1.   We hear much nowadays of the Bible as literature. Plainly our publishers have discovered that the Bible is out and away the greatest book of English prose, and are determined that we shall read it for its splendours of expression, if for nothing else. One is reminded of the story told by T. R. Glover of an eminent English poet. One morning his wife invaded his study and set him to read a 'portion of God's Word'. He obeyed, and a little later when his son came in and saw what he was reading, the poet looked up and said, 'My boy, you should always read the Bible; there's nothing like it for your style.' Does this story contain the reason why we should read the New Testament? Is it for its literary interest that we should study it well, especially as it comes to most of us in the glorious English of the forty-seven men who made the Authorized Version?

No; as a matter of fact, from a purely literary point of view, the New Testament is vastly inferior to that other volume which is usually, and rightly, bound up

with it, and which we call the Old Testament. (If you
examine any collection of great English prose—as, for
example, Logan Pearsall Smith's *Treasury of English
Prose*—you will see that the literary man finds far more
to praise in the Old Testament than he does in the New.)
To be sure, there are not a few passages in the New
Testament which for sheer beauty hold an unchallenge-
able place in the world's literature. Where will you find
a short story more movingly and exquisitely told than
in the Parable of the Prodigal Son? Where a nobler
prose-poem than the thirteenth chapter of First Corinthians? Where a finer piece of pure eloquence than the
roll-call of the heroes of faith in the eleventh chapter of
Hebrews? Nevertheless, it is not for this reason that we
bid men turn to the New Testament. It is true that a
man may begin by studying the New Testament with a
purely literary concern and end up by studying it for
some quite other and deeper reason, as Augustine in his
preconversion days went to hear Ambrose preach in
Milan, interested not in *what* Ambrose said but in *how*
he said it; and, by and by, had to confess that while he
opened his heart 'to admit the eloquence of his
utterances, there gradually entered likewise a conviction
of the truth of what he said'. Yet it is not as literature,
not for its style primarily, that we ask men to reckon
with this book.

2. Is it, then, for its pure and lofty moral teaching?
Christianity being admittedly a method of goodness—
God's way of making men good—is it because we have
in the New Testament a matchless guide-book to the
good life that men ought to study it? Is it as the world's
supreme text-book on ethics that the New Testament

commands the attention of all interested in the problem of right living?

This is the answer of some. But if the peculiar virtue of the New Testament lies in its ethics, clearly three-fourths of it must be regarded as irrelevant. For, since most of the pure gold of the New Testament's ethical teaching is to be found in the Sermon on the Mount, one or two chapters of St Paul, the Epistle of James, and a few other passages, we must (on this view) con-clude that the bulk of the New Testament is, for all practical purposes, so much literary dross which we may safely throw away. Some people think this is what ought to be done. They lavish their praise on the Ser-mon on the Mount, and on the thirteenth chapter of First Corinthians; but they can only regret that these ethical treasures come to us embedded in a fantastic framework of myth and supernaturalism. What we ought to do (say they), is to conserve this precious ethical residuum at all costs, and consign the myth and miracle to the limbo of forgotten things. Thus Dr Klausner, the eminent Jewish scholar, would like to preserve 'the book of the ethics of Jesus' (presumably the great Sermon) after ridding it of its 'wrappings of miracle and mysticism'.[1] And that fine-minded humanist, the late Dr Gilbert Murray, was apparently of much the same way of thinking.

Of course no Christian man could ever countenance this proposal. To jettison all the miracle and mysticism would be to jettison most of what makes the New Testament precious to him; and while he may feel a bit uneasy about some of the miracles, he realizes that a New Testament containing only a few selected ethical

[1] *Jesus of Nazareth*, p. 414.

passages would be something very like *Hamlet* with the Prince of Denmark left out. Besides, a very casual knowledge of the New Testament tells him that this proposed purge of the New Testament is quite impracticable; for whether we like it or not, the ethics of the New Testament are inseparably bound up with its religion (which includes miracle and mysticism); and, in short, the notion that we can wander through the New Testament, as through a garden, plucking here and there an ethical flower for the adornment of our philosophy of life, is a quite arbitrary procedure. No; the peculiar virtue of the New Testament does not lie in its ethical glories; not for these primarily do we read it.

3.   Others there are who, finding the quintessence of Christianity in 'Christ's views about God and the Sermon on the Mount' (to quote the late Dick Sheppard), think that it is in these that the value of the New Testament lies.[1]

Behind this view lies the assumption that Christianity is 'the last and loftiest construction that man has put on the Infinite'.

The Christian idea of God, for example, is the sublime discovery of that spiritual genius, Jesus of Nazareth, 'the Columbus of the spiritual world who has by searching found out God'. Moreover, in the teaching of this spiritual genius meet all our highest ideas of human conduct. Morality, as we see it in the Sermon on the Mount, has come forth from His hands a new creation, and in it we are to find the noblest expression of man's

[1] This is, in essence, the view of (theological) Liberalism. It values the New Testament because in it we find the highest and purest 'message about God and the good' (the words are Harnack's) uttered by man.

duty on this earth. Because the New Testament is the repository of this sublime teaching about God and man's duty, we ought to study it and prize it above all the religious classics of mankind.

This is, admittedly, some advance on the previous view. Let us not speak scornfully of men who find in the New Testament no more than this. Yet let us also be clear that if it is in 'Christ's views about God and the Sermon on the Mount' that the peculiar virtue of the New Testament lies, then once again most of it ought to go into the waste-paper basket, or be preserved only for its antiquarian value. For the logical consequence of this view is that Paul and all the other New Testament theologians—who found in Christ not simply the spiritual Columbus of our race but in some sense the very God Himself stooping low for our redemption—ought to be dismissed as misguided enthusiasts who turned 'the beautiful idyll of Galilee' into a cosmic drama of salvation. This view, in fact, is contrary to the whole tenor of the New Testament. The New Testament writers never lead us to suppose that the precious thing they have to give us is men's thoughts about God, however sublime; what they claim to give us is God's Word —His final Word—to men about Himself. And now, as the children say, we are really getting hot. . . .

4. For what then (to come to the crux of the matter) are we to study the New Testament?

It is a cardinal canon of all criticism that in dealing with any great work our prime endeavour should be to understand (as the Greeks would say) its *to ti ēn einai*— 'the thing it was to be'. If applying this canon to the New Testament, we ask what the New Testament writers aim to give us, the answer is neither *belles lettres*, nor superfine ethics, nor even lofty views about God, but Good News *from* God—authentic tidings of God's good will made manifest to redeem and deliver sinful men. And to this day, when simple men and women go to the New Testament, this is what they seek. They do not seek fine literature: they can get that elsewhere, in Shakespeare and many another. They do not seek merely moral light and leading: they can get that in the writings of many a good and wise man of this world. They do not even seek views about God: they can get these in any handbook of comparative religion. They seek news of what Karl Barth calls 'a vertical miracle'. Beset behind and before with sin and guilt, perplexed and bewildered by the burden and mystery of life, they seek 'a Word from the Beyond for our human predicament'. And it is just because the New Testament is, from the Gospels to the Apocalypse, one triumphant testimony that God has spoken this Word that it occupies a place of solitary splendour in the literature of the world. That is to say, the importance of the New Testament is that it claims to be the record of a unique self-revelation of the living God on the stage of human history.

That revelation may be summed up in various ways:

'God was in Christ reconciling the world unto Himself.'

'The Word became flesh and dwelt among us.'

'God . . . hath at the end of these days spoken unto us in His Son.'

But, however varied be the expression, it is always the

record of the inconceivable condescension of God to us men in the person of Jesus Christ, His Son.

No other set of religious books in all the world makes this astonishing and tremendous claim. Nowhere else do we find documents purporting to record a 'vertical miracle' like this. As an American scholar has finely phrased it: 'If there be any true myth, if the Divine Nature has at any time and in any wise revealed itself to men, if any voice shall ever reach us out of the infinite circle of silence, where else shall we look for it but to the words of the Gospel?'

There are three things to be said of this revelation and its record:

First, it is a revelation that comes by action rather than by words, by deeds rather than by doctrines. This is just to say that it is the revelation of 'the living God', the God who is known by what He does, the God whose character is to be discerned in the stuff of history. We remember Goethe's great saying: 'The highest cannot be spoken; it can only be acted.' It is the claim of the New Testament that the All Highest has once for all acted in a special series of events in history—the coming of Christ—in such a way as to show men for ever what He is like.

> 'Here His whole Name appears complete;
>   Nor wit can guess, nor reason prove,
> Which of the letters best is writ,
>   The Power, the Wisdom, or the Love.'

Second, to claim that the New Testament enshrines a unique self-revelation of God is not to say that God may not reveal Himself generally in other ways. Indeed, you will find in the New Testament several passages which declare, or imply, that God has not left Himself without witness in nature and history, apart altogether from the revelation in Christ. But the New Testament writers do insist that in the record of God's dealings with a special People, the Jews, given us in the Bible, and culminating in the coming of Christ, and the creation of a new People of God which is the Christian Church, we have history as a process of Divine Self-revelation (what the Germans call *Heilsgeschichte*).

Third, it is because the Bible, with the New Testament as its climax and crown, is the record of that revelation, that we say it 'contains' the Word of God. The matter has never been better expressed than by Robertson Smith when he stood arraigned for heresy: 'If I am asked why I receive scripture as the Word of God, I answer with all the Fathers of the Protestant Church: Because the Bible is the only record of the redeeming Love of God, because in the Bible alone I find God drawing near to man in Christ Jesus and declaring to us, in Him, His will for our salvation. And this record I know to be true by the witness of His Spirit in my heart whereby I am assured that none other than God Himself is able to speak such words to my soul.'

II

Language, Text and Canon

BEFORE we 'clap into it roundly', there are three preliminary questions to be answered:

In what language was the New Testament originally written?

Can we be sure that we have the New Testament books substantially as they left the writers' hands?

How came the twenty-seven books of the New Testament to be gathered together and accepted as authoritative Christian scripture?

1. All the New Testament books were originally written in Greek. On the face of it, this may surprise us. Aramaic, a language akin to Hebrew, was the mother-tongue of Jesus; and though He may have been able to speak Greek, it was in Aramaic, not Greek, that He preached and taught. Further, the masters of the civilized world in those days were the Romans, and we might have expected that their language would have been the tongue in which the New Testament books (addressed as they were to subjects of Rome) would have been written. Why then did St Paul (for example) use Greek and not Latin when he wrote to the Christians in Rome? And if the language of the New Testament was Greek, what sort of Greek was it? Four or five centuries before Christ came, Plato had philosophized in Greek, Demosthenes made speeches in Greek, Sophocles written plays in Greek. Did Paul, Luke, John

and the rest of the New Testament writers use the same Greek as they?

The answer is, Yes and No. The language they used was Greek, but it was by no means the same Greek as men had used in the days of 'the glory that was Greece'. Their Greek we call 'classical Greek'; the Greek of the New Testament writers we call 'common Greek'. Not that, though simpler, it was necessarily poor or bad: it is called 'common' because it was in common use: it was Greek 'in widest commonalty spread'.

This common Greek was, in the time of Christ and the apostles, the international language of the age. One man had played a main part in making it so: Alexander of Macedon. Not only did Alexander, in the fourth century B.C., conquer a great part of the civilized world, but he took with him his language wherever his armies marched; and what had once been the tongue of a small country became the international tongue of a large portion of the known world, from the gates of India to the proud city of Rome, and all round the Mediterranean.

It was in this international language, Common Greek, that the heralds of the Gospel preached when they 'turned to the Gentiles', and in this language that the New Testament writers wrote the Gospels and Epistles.

Only one qualification needs to be made. The language of the New Testament was common Greek plus 'a Semitic somewhat'. Readers of Bunyan know that he is one of the great masters of Saxon prose. Yet his prose is not simply Saxon prose; it is Saxon prose with 'a Biblical accent'. New Testament Greek is common Greek with 'a Semitic accent'—with a Hebraic tincture in phrase and idiom. This is what we might have expected; for all the New Testament writers, with the exception of Luke, were Jews—men whose 'background' was Hebraic, men who had been nurtured on the Jewish scriptures.

So, the original language of the New Testament was the common vernacular Greek of the Roman world in the first century A.D. (the language in which the numerous papyrus letters and documents, recently dug up in Egypt, are written): a simple, flexible, and (as Moffatt says) 'eminently translatable' speech, lacking indeed some of the beauty and delicacy of 'classical Greek', yet surely, under the providence of God, a far more suitable medium for proclaiming the Good News to those that were 'afar off'—the 'not many wise, not many mighty, not many noble', whom Paul and his coadjutors did not disdain to enlist in the Kingdom of God.

2. Eighteen centuries have passed since the New Testament books were written, and inevitably the question arises, 'Do we now possess these books in anything like their original form?'

We do not, of course, now possess 'the originals', or 'autographs', as they are called. These have perished. But we can be tolerably sure of what they must have looked like. All of them were probably papyrus rolls. The papyrus (from which comes our word 'paper') is an aquatic plant of the sedge family which grew abundantly in marshy spots like the Nile Delta. When the old paper-makers set to work, their first task was to extract the pith from the papyrus reeds and to cut it into fine strips. They laid some of the strips side by side vertically and then crossed them horizontally with other strips to form a page generally about ten inches long and five inches broad. These rough sheets were then soaked in water and treated with gum, and after being dried in the sun and polished with an ivory roller were ready for use. (Countless such sheets have been dug up from the sands of Upper Egypt during the last half century.) All you needed now if you wished to write was a reed pen cut with a pen-knife into the proper shape, and some ink made from soot, gum and water. If you had some skill at it, you would do your own writing; or you might, as St Paul often did, dictate to a scribe and add your own signature at the end to authenticate your letter.

A single papyrus sheet would suffice for a short note like St Paul's Epistle to Philemon. For longer compositions like St Luke's Gospel, you had to join many of these sheets together to form a roll, perhaps thirty feet long. If you meant your writing to be read often, you would furnish your roll with a stick at each end for winding and unwinding.

Such must have been the format of the New Testament autographs. But if these have perished, can we be confident that we know what was written on them? After all, for almost fourteen hundred years (roughly 100–1454)—the years between the writing of the New Testament and the invention of printing—the New Testament was copied by hand. To err is human, and copying by hand perforce produces a crop of errors. No scribe, however expert in his craft, can avoid mistakes. No later copyist finding such mistakes is likely to resist the temptation to try to correct his predecessor's slips. Thus errors are produced and perpetuated. Since the New Testament text ran these risks for so many centuries, can we be sure that the best text we have to-day is anything like what the original writers wrote?

There is reason for confidence. Not only can we detect and explain most of the errors, but by using a threefold chain of evidence we can show that the text of the New Testament which existed in the second century was for all practical purposes identical with the text (the Greek text) which underlies the Revised Version of the New Testament.

What is this threefold chain?

(1) The great Greek manuscripts. The oldest of them, being written in block capitals, are styled 'uncials'; and the later ones 'cursives', because the letters are ligatured together as in our modern running script. Among the 'uncials', which are the more important, are Codex Vaticanus (or B), Codex Sinaiticus (or S), and Codex Bezae (or D). The first two go back to the fourth century, the third to the fifth.

(2) The Versions, i.e. early translations of the Greek New Testament into other languages. Of these the most important are those in Latin and in Syriac (the language of ancient Syria, a Western dialect of Aramaic). A study of these proves that a text very like that in the oldest Greek manuscripts must have existed not later than the middle of the second century A.D.

(3) Quotations of the New Testament in the early Church Fathers, e.g. Tatian who composed a harmony of the Gospels about A.D. 170. True, the value of this last evidence is often vitiated by the fact that the Fathers did not always quote accurately; still, they are evidence that the New Testament, from the end of the second century on, stood practically in its present form.

Such are the materials for reconstructing the original text of the New Testament; and when we remember

how meagre are the materials for the text of many of
the great Greek and Latin writers (we have only two
manuscripts of Catullus), we realize that the scholars
who work on the text of the New Testament suffer
almost from an embarrassment of riches. (We possess
about three thousand Greek manuscripts of the whole
or parts of the New Testament.) Into the intricacies of
their science we cannot enter here, but we can sum up
the results of their labours in the words of two of the
greatest of them: 'The words in our opinion still subject
to doubt can hardly amount to more than a thousandth
part of the New Testament' (Westcott and Hort). In
short, the 1881 Revised Version of the New Testament,
which is based on a much better knowledge of the
manuscripts than the Authorized Version of 1611, and
was made under the influence of the two great textual
scholars just named, gives us a translation based on a
text which is as near to what the original writers wrote,
as makes no important difference.

3.   The third question in this chapter concerns the
Canon. The word which meant originally a 'reed' or
'cane', later 'a measuring-rod' and so a 'standard' or
'rule', signifies here the list of sacred books accepted by
the Church as authoritative in matters of faith and life.
The question before us now is: How came these twenty-
seven books in the New Testament to achieve that
authority?

Jesus Christ wrote nothing; and when the little People
of God started on its great career, the only scripture the
Christians had was the Old Testament which in the
light of recent events—the coming of Jesus the Messiah
—had become a new book for them. But alongside the

Old Testament stood 'the Words of the Lord' (cf. Acts 20.35; I Cor. 7.10) and the story of His ministry first committed to writing about A.D. 65, to be followed in the next thirty years by the other three Gospels. At first these Gospels would circulate locally, but later they gained a wider currency. Before, however, the earliest Gospel appeared, Paul was writing letters to his churches. These would be read publicly, and afterwards lent to sister churches and copies made of them; so that by the end of the first century little collections of Paul's letters came into existence. Then other letters associated with the names of apostolic men—e.g. the Epistles of John—appeared and were similarly prized. So, book by book, the New Testament began to emerge. Not that only our New Testament books were in circulation: there were others like *The Shepherd of Hermas* (a sort of early *Pilgrim's Progress*) and some highly fanciful Gospels and Acts designed to fill in gaps in the early Christians' knowledge of the Lord and His apostles. (These latter make up what is known nowadays as 'The Apocryphal New Testament', as *The Shepherd* and some other similar books constitute 'The Apostolic Fathers'.)

But how were our twenty-seven books raised to canonical rank?

To begin with, the process was largely informal and unofficial. We err if we imagine a committee of venerable ecclesiastics sitting down round a table with several piles of books on it (Gospels, Epistles, etc.) and gravely weighing the merits of each book until finally they had a little pile of twenty-seven ready for official publication. Councils and committees played a very small part in the business.

In the next place, the process of inclusion and exclusion was gradual. The New Testament did not suddenly spring into being like Athene from the head of Zeus. Something like three hundred years elapsed before the scattered writings were collected into the New Testament as we know it to-day.

The history of the formation of the Canon is long and (truth to tell) rather dull. We shall content ourselves with picking out two salient dates. By the year 200 the main contents of the New Testament had been decided. Only seven of our twenty-seven books—Hebrews, James, Jude, II Peter, II and III John, and Revelation —remained in doubt. (We know this from a fragmentary document called 'The Muratorian Canon' which lists the books deemed canonical in the Church of Rome at the time.) The other date is 367, the year in which Athanasius (better known as the champion of orthodoxy at Nicea) defined, in a famous letter, a canon of twenty-seven books which corresponds exactly with the New Testament as we have it to-day. After that it only remained for various councils to ratify decisions already reached by the good sense of the Church at large.

What causes compelled the Church to form a canon?

One was the emergence of a host of Christian writings of dubious value and authority: the Church had to decide which books contained true Christian tradition and teaching. More potent perhaps was the infiltration into the Church of heresies like Gnosticism: if the Church was to guard her members against this false teaching, necessity was laid on her to repudiate all such paganizing of the Faith, and to say where sound doctrine was to be found.

Public lection and apostolicity were the main guiding

principles in the choice of canonical books. That is to say, the two criteria were (*a*) the fact that a book was regularly read in Church; and (*b*) the belief that it emanated from apostolic circles. 'These two tests of canonicity', it has been well said, 'are an attempt to make sure that the book has something to say to the Church, and that what it says really originates from the circle to whom the revelation in Jesus Christ was given.'[1]

Comparing the books now included in the Canon with those that were excluded, we cannot doubt that here, as in other matters, the early Church showed a sanctified common sense. They were tried money-changers (as their Lord is said to have bidden them be) proving all things and holding fast that which was good.

[1] T. W. Manson, *A Companion to the Bible*, p. 11 f.

III

The Contents of the New Testament

THE New Testament is really Volume Two in the story of salvation which is the theme of the whole Bible. It tells how, when the decisive hour of history struck, God fulfilled the great promises made to the men of the old covenant by visiting and redeeming His People in His Son Jesus who was the Messiah; and how the new People of God, which is the Christian Church, went forth to spread the news of that salvation in the wider world.

The New Testament comprises twenty-seven books; but some are very short; and, altogether, the New Testament is only about a third of the length of the Old Testament. These twenty-seven books we may classify and characterize as follows:

First, we have four documents called 'Gospels' which, at first blush, look like biographies of Jesus but which, on closer perusal, hardly answer to our modern notions of biographical writing. Then comes a volume of history (really a sequel to the Third Gospel): The Acts of the Apostles. Then follow twenty-one documents which our Bible comprehensively labels 'Epistles'; though that term we find is very elastic, and covers many literary types, from a massive theological treatise (Romans) to a charming little private letter (Philemon), and includes a rhetorical homily (Hebrews) and an ethical scrap-book (James); and the whole is rounded off with a book of visions named 'The Revelation of St John the Divine'.

To this collection of twenty-seven books Paul, who has fourteen Epistles[1] ascribed to him, and Luke, who wrote both the Gospel bearing his name and Acts, are the two chief contributors; but modern scholarship counts some dozen different authors in the whole New Testament.

In our New Testament the books are not arranged chronologically. Chronologically, Paul's Epistles ought to stand first, with either Galatians or First Thessalonians at their head. As for the Gospels, Mark should come first and John last. Further, not Revelation (which was written about A.D. 95) but Second Peter should, if we studied strict chronology, stand last in the Canon. In this book, however, we are going to study the reader's convenience by considering the books in the general order in which they appear in the Bible: Gospels, Epistles, Apocalypse—an order which, in spiritual logic, can be justified entirely; for Matthew, the first Gospel, with its emphasis on Jesus as the fulfiller of the old covenant, helps to bind together the two Testaments, and Revelation, coming at the end, supplies a perfect *dénouement* to the story of salvation with its message of the judgment and victory of God.

Our first section will deal with the four Gospels. After considering how the Gospels came into existence, we shall go on to discuss the literary connexion between the first three (the Synoptic problem) and conclude with a chapter on each of the four.

The subject of the second section will be 'The Early Church and St Paul'. We need to remember that (as

---

[1] One of them, *Hebrews*, certainly erroneously, as we shall see.

Luke says) the Gospels tell us only what 'Jesus began
to do and to teach'. The resurrection is not the end of
the story. The acts of Christ did not cease there; they
were continued in the acts of His Apostles. Our first
study therefore in this section will be the book which
forms the bridge between the Gospels and the rest of
the New Testament, namely, the Acts of the Apostles,
or, as we have called it, 'How they (the Apostles)
brought the Good News from Jerusalem to Rome.' Of
the Apostles we know most about St Paul, and to his
life we shall devote a chapter, not only because the story
of it is intrinsically important, but because it supplies a
framework into which we can dovetail his letters. Paul's
letters fall into three classes: (1) Travel Epistles:
Galatians, I and II Thessalonians, I and II Corinthians
and Romans; (2) Prison Epistles: Ephesians, Colossians,
Philemon and Philippians; and (3) the Pastoral Epistles:
I and II Timothy and Titus.

Our third section will deal with 'The Writings of the
other Apostolic Men'.

Finally, to round off the whole, we have added an
epilogue called, 'The Unity of the New Testament',
which tries to express in briefest compass the central
theme of the New Testament.

PART TWO

THE FOUR GOSPELS

IV

How the Gospels came to be Written

GOSPEL, a fine old English word from 'god spel', i.e. good news, translates the Greek word *euangelion*.

Originally, this Greek word meant the reward given to a man who brought 'good news'. Then it came to mean the good news itself. Then—and this is the New Testament sense—it came to signify the Good News proclaimed by and centring in Jesus. Later still, it was applied to canonical 'memoirs' of Jesus. With this last meaning we reach the common usage of to-day. By the Gospels we mean written records of the Good News which came into the world with the coming of Jesus Christ; for Jesus, as Dr Dale said truly, came not simply to preach the Gospel, but that there might be a Gospel to preach.

Life always precedes literature, and we do well to remember that the Good News was being proclaimed before any Christian literature existed at all. In the first generation of Christianity (roughly A.D. 30–60) there were no written Gospels (the only scripture the first Christians had was the Old Testament), but there was a *kerygma*. This Greek word means a (preached) 'message', and thanks to the researches of modern scholars we can form a rough idea of its contents.

A careful comparison of the speeches in the early chapters of the Acts (e.g. Acts 10.36-43) with certain passages in St Paul's Epistles where he is clearly handling traditional material (e.g. I Cor. 15.3 ff.) yields an outline of the 'message' which formed the earliest Good News. It ran somewhat as follows:

God's promises made to His People in the Old Testament are now fulfilled.

The long-expected Messiah, born of David's line, has come.

He is Jesus of Nazareth, who

went about doing good and wrought mighty works by God's power;

was crucified according to the purpose of God;

was raised by God from the dead and exalted to His right hand.

He will come again in glory for judgment.

Therefore let all who hear this message repent and be baptized for the forgiveness of their sins.

In the beginning, then, was the *kerygma*, and this 'message' was the earliest Gospel, with which the apostles, or 'messengers', of Christ went forth (as they said in Thessalonica) to 'turn the whole world upsidedown'. There might be differences of emphasis in this early preaching according as it was addressed primarily to Jews or Gentiles; but the core of it was the same: 'Whether then it be I or they (the Jerusalem apostles),' said Paul, 'it was thus we preached and thus ye believed' (I Cor. 15.11). The earliest Gospel, as we need sometimes to remind ourselves, was not the Sermon on the Mount or any similar moral manifesto, but a story about the Cross on the hill and the empty grave, and the 'mighty acts of God' made manifest therein.

But, of course, the bare outline given above must have been filled in by the earliest preachers; and if we ask with what, the answer is: with stories about Jesus. There was no lack of these; for many still lived who had seen Jesus in the days of His flesh, or knew those who had companied with Him, and could tell stories of His wonderful deeds: how He had healed the sick, or blessed little children, or fed a great multitude, or silenced a Pharisaic critic, or, on the last evening with His disciples, made broken bread and out-poured wine symbolize His approaching death. Indeed, it is probable that in every great centre of early Christianity—Jerusalem, Antioch, Caesarea, Rome—there must have grown up cycles of stories about Jesus, which the 'saints' passed from one to another at their common meals or when they met for worship, and which the apostolic preachers used in their sermons. At this stage, then, memories were still fresh, and no clamant need was yet felt for written records of Jesus.

But what of the teaching of Jesus? The outline of the *kerygma* given above says little or nothing about this. Yet we should err if we imagined that the early Christians forgot or ignored all the memorable sayings of Him who spake as never man spake. On the contrary, we know that these sayings were treasured for the guidance they gave on the problems of Christian life and practice. St Paul, for example, was not ignorant of what Jesus had said, and from time to time (see e.g. I Cor. 7.10; 11.23 ff.; Acts 20.35) would quote 'words of the Lord' to settle hard questions in his churches. So we may be sure that from the beginning men remembered the *dicta* of Jesus, prizing them no doubt for their own sake—because they were the words of their exalted

Lord—but also, as we have just seen, for their practical value. And by and by, a collection of these sayings of Jesus was made to serve as a guide to Christian behaviour for those who by accepting the apostolic 'message' had become Christians.[1]

So the materials later to be woven into our written Gospels took shape during the generation that followed the Crucifixion and Resurrection. This is the period of *the oral tradition*—the period when men still preferred 'the living and abiding voice' of eyewitnesses to any written record of Jesus. It is a time when, as Dr Vincent Taylor has put it, 'precious fragments are treasured for their immediate interest and value; Christian hands are full of jewels, but there is no desire to weave a crown'.[2]

That time was to come. A generation had gone past since Jesus had died and risen; a generation in which 'the hallowed fire' of the Gospel flew from Jerusalem to Rome. Many of the eyewitnesses had now 'fallen asleep'; some had been killed. It became increasingly important that the facts about Jesus should be set down in writing before the time should come when there would be none left able to say: 'I remember Jesus Christ.' Besides, converts were flocking into the young churches; converts who needed instruction in the Christian Faith. In short, the need for a written record of the Lord Jesus began to be urgently felt, and with the need came the man.

That man was Mark. He it was who wrote the earliest Gospel. What materials lay to his hand? To begin with, he had an outline of the Lord's ministry in the *kerygma* —a rough and ready outline, to be sure, but one that

[1] See next chapter.
[2] *The Formation of the Gospel Tradition*, p. 175.

could be filled out with the stories of Jesus. He had probably his own memories of Jesus during His last week in Jerusalem; he had many more stories which he had got from his friend Peter; and, of course, there were many other stories current in the Christian circles in which he moved. With these Mark wove his crown. That was somewhere about A.D. 65. With the appearance of Mark's Gospel the period of the oral tradition is at an end, and the written period begins. In the next thirty years three other men whom we know as Matthew, Luke, and John were to follow his example, and all of them (as we shall see) were, in greater or less degree, debtors to John Mark.

V

The Synoptic Problem: A Literary Puzzle

THE first three Gospels are commonly called 'the Synoptic Gospels' because they give a synopsis, or common outline, of the story of Jesus. Place the contents of these Gospels side by side in columns, and you will soon become aware of 'the Synoptic problem'. The problem is posed by the remarkable parallelism existing among the first three Gospels. You might not be surprised to find the same incidents described in three different biographies of some great person; what is strange in the first three Gospels is to find the same incidents in the story of Jesus described in practically the same language. These similarities are just those which, if they occurred in three different newspapers, you would attribute to their having one or more special correspondents in common, whose dispatches had been freely edited. We infer that each of these Gospels, though independently written, must have drawn much of its materials from a source, or sources, available to one or both of the others. To discover these sources is the task set by the Synoptic problem.

The first attempt at a solution was the oral tradition theory. Behind the three Gospels (it was said) lay a common oral tradition about Jesus, more or less fixed so far as the core was concerned. This solution is now abandoned because it fails to explain the minute linguistic resemblances among the Synoptic Gospels. (Compare Matt. 9.6; Mark 2.10; Luke 5.24, where a paltry parenthesis—'he said to the paralytic'—is found to be common to all three.) Only a documentary theory (we now realize) will fit facts like these. In other words, if very similar matter occurs in one or more evangelists, we must attribute it to their common use of one or more written sources.

An explanation of this sort is now generally accepted. It is called 'the two document theory', and it holds that two basic documents underlie the Synoptic Gospels. They are our Mark and a sayings-source called Q (German, *Quelle*: source).

The first principle of this theory is:

The Priority of Mark

By this it is meant that the earliest account of Christ's ministry is to be found in Mark, and that Mark was used as one of their main sources by Matthew and Luke.

In support of this view, scholars marshal various arguments. Here are three:

(a) Common subject-matter

Matthew contains nearly all Mark (some 606 of Mark's 661 verses reappear in Matthew), and Luke about one half of Mark.

(b) Common Wording

Matthew and Luke often repeat the exact words of Mark—in fact, Matthew reproduces fifty-one per cent, and Luke fifty-three per cent of Mark's language.

(*c*) Common order

Matthew and Luke largely follow Mark's order of events; and when one of them departs from it, the other keeps to it.

The cumulative force of these and other considerations compels us to conclude that the first of the sources used by Matthew and Luke was Mark.

The second principle of the two document theory is:

The Probability of Q

Both Matthew and Luke contain many verses not in Mark. Over two hundred of these they have in common, often in identical language, and these mostly sayings of Jesus. (Compare Matt. 3.7-10 and Luke 3.7-9, or Matt. 11.25-27 and Luke 10.21-22.) This almost certainly indicates the use by Matthew and Luke of a second written source, nowadays invariably called Q.

Q, alas, has not survived; but by comparing these similar verses in Matthew and Luke we can roughly reconstruct it. When this is done, we find that Q must have comprised mainly sayings of Jesus, and almost certainly did not contain the story of the Passion. Much of Q can be recovered from the great Sermon which both Matthew and Luke attribute to Jesus; and from Jesus' charge to His disciples when He sent them out on their mission. Dr T. W. Manson[1] thinks that Q was arranged in four sections:

> Jesus and John the Baptist.
> Jesus and His disciples.
> Jesus and His opponents.
> Sayings about the Last Things.

[1] See *The Sayings of Jesus.*

If we ask what was the purpose of Q, the answer is that it seems to have been a manual of moral instruction for converts. As to its compiler, we can make a scientific guess. A Church Father called Papias, who wrote very early in the second century, declared (according to Eusebius):

'Matthew compiled the *Logia* in the Hebrew (Aramaic?) language and everyone translated them as he was able.'

The *Logia* cannot be our Matthew, which is not a translation from Hebrew or Aramaic. The word might refer to 'Testimonies', that is, Old Testament Messianic proof-texts, of which there are many in Matthew; but, as *Logia* can mean 'oracular utterances', many think that Papias referred to the dominical utterances gathered together in Q. Q's strong interest in the Gentiles has led many to think of Antioch, the cradle of Gentile Christianity, as its place of origin. Its date may be as early as A.D. 50.

Matter peculiar to Matthew and Luke

When we have detached from Matthew and Luke all the materials derived from Mark, we find that each of these evangelists has still much matter peculiar to himself.

Matthew, for example, has more than three hundred verses of his own, containing besides the Birth stories (1–2) some narratives (e.g. Peter's walking on the water, Judas's suicide, and Pilate's hand-washing) and much teaching of Jesus (e.g. large portions of the Sermon on the Mount). The Jewish colouring of much of this material suggests Jerusalem as a place of origin.

As for 'special Luke', we find in the Third Gospel

more than four hundred verses, many of them in the section Luke 9.51–18.14. This includes many narratives (e.g. the sermon at Nazareth, the woman who was a sinner, the walk to Emmaus) and much valuable teaching (e.g. the parables of the Good Samaritan, the Prodigal Son and the Pharisee and the Publican). It is a fair conjecture that Luke gathered this special matter at Caesarea while St Paul was imprisoned there (A.D. 57–59).

Mark, Q, Special Matthew and Special Luke—these are the four strata of tradition which modern scholarship lays bare in the Synoptic Gospels. The first is to be connected with Rome, and the other three with Antioch, Jerusalem and Caesarea respectively. We need only add that the late Canon Streeter, a great expert on this subject, went a little further and spoke of a four document theory. He believed that besides Mark and Q we should posit two more documents M and L, the first being a Jerusalem-sayings source, the second representing the material peculiar to the Third Gospel. This is possible, but speculative.

Before we close this chapter, let us set forth our conclusions in two different ways:

First, in rhyme:

> 'The problem solved is stated here:
> Our Mark did first of all appear.
> For Luke and Matthew used him both.
> But Luke and Matthew nothing loth
> To add some more, used Q (for Quelle[1])
> And each a special source as well.'

[1] *Quelle* is pronounced Kvellé, but the poetic licence may be pardoned!

Second, in diagram:

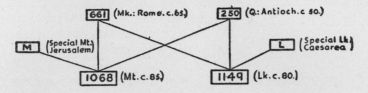

Note

If, after this study of the Synoptic problem, anyone should feel shocked at the literary ethic—or lack of it—which allowed Matthew and Luke to 'crib' from Mark in this barefaced way, let him remember that our law of copyright, a consequence of the invention of printing, did not exist then. In antiquity, when books were copied by hand, commercial copyright had no value, and ancient historians often 'cribbed' portions of their predecessors' work without the courtesy of quotation marks.

VI

The Earliest Gospel

IN 1933 the Reichstag in Berlin was set on fire; and the Nazis, looking round for a suitable scapegoat, fixed the blame on the Communists, many of whom they executed. About nineteen hundred years ago a similar thing happened—in Rome. In the winter of A.D. 64–65 a great fire devastated two-thirds of the city. The mad Emperor Nero, who is said to have been the incendiary, found his scapegoat in the new sect of Christians who were popularly suspected of all sorts of nameless crimes. A 'killing time' ensued, and in it fell two of the Christian leaders named Peter and Paul.[1]

According to tradition (and modern scholars generally agree with it) it was shortly after this that a little book —or, more accurately, a papyrus roll—appeared bearing the title: 'The Gospel of Jesus Christ the Son of God.' It is the book we know as the Gospel according to St Mark. It is our earliest Gospel.

Why was the book written? It was now a full generation since Jesus had died and risen. Even ten years before, Paul says that 'some' of those who had seen Him alive after His Passion had 'fallen asleep', and in the interval many more must have been martyred, or died. It was therefore important that the facts about Jesus should be committed to writing before a time should come when there would be no one left who could say: 'I remember Jesus Christ in the days of His

[1] I owe the substance of this paragraph to Professor Dodd.

flesh. . . .' Besides, the Christians were being persecuted and had to be reminded of their Lord and His sufferings to serve them for example and inspiration in a similar situation. So one day a man called Mark procured some papyrus and set himself to write the earliest Gospel.

The Author

How do we know the name of the first evangelist?

The answer briefly is that all tradition declares the author to have been Mark, and that there is no reason why he should have been so unanimously named as the author unless the tradition were true. Here for example is the earliest bit of testimony transmitted to us, through Eusebius, by Papias, a Christian writer who lived in the first half of the second century:

'Mark, having become the interpreter of Peter, wrote down accurately everything that he remembered without however recording in order what was said or done by Christ.'

And Church Father after Church Father in the next century echoes Papias's testimony. We need therefore have no hesitation in ascribing this Gospel to Mark, about whom happily we know quite a lot.

His full name was John Mark, and he was a native of Jerusalem; for we know that his mother's house became a rendezvous for the leaders of the Jerusalem Church after Pentecost (Acts 12.12). (Perhaps that very house contained the Upper Room of the Last Supper.) If John Mark was not one of the Twelve, we may hazard a confident guess that he knew Jesus during at least the last week of His ministry. Turn up Mark 14.51, and you will read of a mysterious 'young man' who in Gethsemane on the night of the arrest escaped the soldiers' clutches only by leaving behind him the linen garment he was wearing. It is very surprising in the tremendous drama of Christ's last hours to find this trifling detail mentioned at all (Matthew and Luke who copy Mark, omit it). The late Canon Streeter used to say that it was as if a reporter to-day were describing a shocking railway accident—the wild confusion, the telescoped carriages, the groans of the injured and dying—and were blandly to remark, 'Just then Mr John Smith lost his pocket handkerchief.' Just so does the verse in Mark seem to us: it is pointless and inept unless it refers to John Mark himself; unless it is his own modest signature in the corner of his Gospel: his quiet way of saying, 'I was there.'

We have surer information about Mark some years later. Acts tells us that he accompanied Paul and Barnabas (who was his cousin) on their first missionary tour (Acts 13.5, 13). Because Mark deserted them at Perga and went home, Paul refused to take him with them on the second journey, and the two apostles quarrelled. That quarrel, however, must have been composed, for less than ten years later Mark shared Paul's imprisonment in Rome (Col. 4.10-12; Philem. 24; cf. II Tim. 4.11).

But Mark is linked in history not with Paul only but with Peter. In the First Epistle of St Peter there is a tender allusion to 'Mark my son', and the tradition of the Church (as we have seen) is that Mark acted as Peter's interpreter when he preached, and later used the materials so gathered in the composition of his Gospel. No doubt there were other stories about Jesus current in the Church which Mark employed when he came to write his Gospel; but we shall not go far astray if we describe Mark's Gospel as 'reminiscences of Jesus as told by St Peter to his friend John Mark'.

Let us consider these 'reminiscences'.

Mark's Story of Jesus

We can divide Mark's story into four parts: (1) 1.1-13; (2) 1.14–ch. 8; (3) 9–16.8; and (4) 16.9-20.

(1) What we may call the *Prologue* occupies the first thirteen verses of chapter one. In fulfilment of what was said by the Old Testament prophets, John the Baptist appears in the wilderness down near the Dead Sea, calling Israel to repentance and announcing the advent of a mightier than himself. The great day dawns and Jesus comes down from Nazareth and is baptized in Jordan. A divine voice tells Him that He is the Son of God, and He retires into the desert where He is tempted by the devil.

(2) Then, at chapter 1, verse 14, the *first main section* of the Gospel begins. After the Baptist's arrest Jesus comes into Galilee with the startling announcement that the decisive hour of history has struck and that God's Reign has arrived. Let men 'turn again' to God (that is the meaning of 'repent') and believe the glad tidings. He calls two pairs of brothers from their fishing-nets to be His disciples, and entering Capernaum begins to heal and preach. His fame runs like a kindling flame through Galilee. But His claim to forgive sins, His consorting with 'the down-and-outs', His radiant religion, offend the religious leaders; and by and by He is compelled to teach and heal His growing mass of followers by the shores of the Galilean Lake. Twelve men (the nucleus of the New People of God) are appointed to form the inner circle, and serve as His lieutenants in the work of

the Kingdom. His enemies accuse Him of being in league with the powers of evil, and some pronounce Him mad. The Galilean ministry proceeds: He teaches the multitudes about God's Reign in parables, and manifests its presence by mighty works. The Twelve, having been to school with Christ, are now sent forth two by two to tell men about God's Reign and to gather in God's People. When they return, the Galilean ministry reaches its climax in a great mass-feeding of five thousand people. We may call it the Galilean Lord's Supper.

Thereafter Jesus leads the Twelve north-west into the heathen regions of Tyre and Sidon, and on their return journey, at a place called Caesarea Philippi, in the shadow of snow-capped Hermon, a decisive stage in Christ's ministry is reached. Peter, in answer to his Master's leading question, confesses Jesus to be the Messiah, the Saviour for whom the Jews had been waiting for centuries. At once Jesus tells His disciples that if He is the Son of Man (another title for the Messiah) He must go to His throne by way of the gallows. The disciples are shocked and incredulous. From that time onwards the shadow of a cross falls ever more darkly across the story.

(3) So ends the first main section of Mark's Gospel. The *second main section* which covers chapters 9–16.8, carries the story of Jesus down to the cross and its sequel.

Six days after Peter's confession Jesus is transfigured on a mountain-top before three of His disciples; and henceforward the whole story moves towards Jerusalem where Jesus goes to die. Passing through Galilee to Capernaum, He travels south through Perea to Judea, until He reaches Jericho. And as He travels, we see Him healing demoniacs and blind men, blessing little children, answering the Pharisees, and all the while preparing His disciples for the Cross. From Jericho He passes to Bethany, two miles from Jerusalem.

Then follow all the events which we associate with Holy Week: the triumphal entry and the cleansing of the Temple (both 'action sermons'); the teaching in the Temple[1] and the anointing at Bethany. Finally, on the Thursday night, He holds the Last Supper in an upper room of Jerusalem, endures the Agony in Gethsemane, is arrested, tried and condemned. On Friday morning at 9 a.m. He is lifted up on a cross, and at 3 p.m. He dies. Some hours later, a secret disciple, Joseph of Arimathea, with the consent of the Roman Governor buries the body decently in a rock-tomb. It is Friday evening and the story of Jesus seems at an end.

But no; there is a sequel, an astounding sequel. On the Sunday morning, as we should say, some women going to anoint Jesus' body find the tomb empty, and a mysterious young man declares: 'He is not here. He is risen.' Awe-stricken, the women flee from the scene.

(4) At this point Mark's Gospel comes to an abrupt end. If our earliest and best manuscripts are to be trusted, *The Epilogue*, Mark 16.9-20, in our Bibles is by another and later hand. (Did Mark mean to end here? Or was he interrupted before he could finish? Or, likeliest of all, has the last page of his Gospel been accidentally torn off?) It tells how the risen Jesus appeared again to His disciples and commanded them to preach the Gospel to all creation.

[1] Mark 13, the only long discourse in Mark, is regarded by many scholars as an apocalyptic 'tract' (containing a few genuine sayings of Jesus) which was current in the Church and found its way into the earliest Gospel.

The Characteristics of the Earliest Gospel

What are the main impressions which a reading of the earliest Gospel leaves with the reader?

First, perhaps, there is the rough but vivid vigour of Mark's style. Mark is not a man of letters; but he is one of those persons who, though they may tear grammar to tatters, can tell a story graphically. His narrative abounds with vivid little touches such as he could only have got from one like Peter who had been an eyewitness. We see Jesus take the children in the crook of His arms—asleep on the rower's cushion in the fishing-boat—looking with love on the rich young man—striding on ahead of the disciples, a great lonely figure, on the road to Jerusalem.

Next, possibly, it is Mark's realism that impresses us. 'Sir, we would see Jesus,' the Greeks once said to Philip. Mark shows us Jesus, as no other evangelist does, in all His gracious humanity. We see one who is bone of our bone and flesh of our flesh, hungry, grieved, happy, sad: one who is touched with the feeling of our infirmities, one who sorrows even unto death: in short, a real man like us in all respects save sin; so that, as we read, we say with Pilate of old, 'Behold the Man!'

But if we stopped there, we should have told only half the truth. If Mark paints for us the man Jesus, he also paints for us the strong Son of God. It is not only true that a divine voice at the Baptism (and again at the Transfiguration) proclaims Him such, or that Jesus Himself in the parable of the wicked husbandmen makes that tremendous claim. Through the whole story there runs 'a mysterious undercurrent' which, as Professor Dodd says, reminds us that the story is more than that of a mere martyrdom. There is a mystery about this Man. He speaks as none other ever spoke. He possesses powers which no other man ever had. He knows that He is doing a work for 'the many' which He alone can do. He speaks of His death as inaugurating a new order of relations between God and men. When, therefore, we read that the grave could not hold Him, we feel that this is the only fitting *dénouement* to the story.

For the story is not simply that of 'one more unfortunate gone to his death' through the malice of men, nor even of one more prophet or reformer sealing his testimony to the truth, as God gives him to see it, with his life's blood. It is the story of how God's Kingdom— His saving Rule—was once and for all manifested in His only Son Jesus the Messiah, and realized 'with power' by His resurrection from the dead.

For sheer beauty of narrative we shall go to the Gospel according to St Luke. For profound insight into the eternal significance of the Gospel we shall prefer St John. For a systematic presentation of Christ's teaching (here Mark is deficient) we shall read St Matthew. But for the earliest, simplest and shortest record of the strong Son of God 'who was manifested' (as the collect has it) 'that He might destroy the works of the devil and make us the sons of God and heirs of life eternal', there is but one book. Long neglected by the Church, the Gospel according to St Mark has now again, thanks to the scholars, come into its own as the primary 'life' of Jesus, and its author, all desertion of St Paul forgiven, stands out in history as

'The saint who first found grace to pen
The life which was the Life of men.'

VII

The Gentile Christian Gospel

THERE is a story told of the late Principal Denney that, being asked one day by an American student to recommend 'a good life of Christ', he fixed him with a quizzical glance and answered with a question, 'Have you read the one by St Luke?' For many, 'the one by St Luke' is the best that has ever been written; they acclaim it (with Renan) as 'the most beautiful book in the world'. This is the book which, for reasons which will appear, we call 'The Gospel for the Gentiles.'

The first point to seize, however, is that this Gospel is really Part I of a two-volumed work. Some years ago there was published a massive work in five volumes entitled *The Beginnings of Christianity*. If the title is modern, the idea is almost nineteen hundred years old; for the first writer in this field was the man who gave us the two biggest books in the New Testament: the Gospel according to St Luke and the Acts of the Apostles. These are not two separate and unconnected works; they are linked together by their style, their prefaces, and by their subject-matter. In fact, they are two volumes on the same theme, and if the author were publishing his work to-day, the full title would read something like this: *The Beginnings of Christianity* (in two volumes) by Dr Luke. Vol. I, The Story of how the Good News began with Jesus in Galilee and Jerusalem. Vol. II, How His Apostles carried the Good News from Jerusalem to Rome.

Volume II will concern us later. Our immediate interest is Volume I.

Who wrote the Third Gospel?

What evidence have we for holding that Luke wrote the Gospel bearing his name?

First, a comparison of the opening verses of Luke (1.1-4) with the preface of Acts (1.1 f.), and a study of the style of the two books leave no room for doubt that they were written by the same man.

Second, certain extracts from a travel-diary in Acts (the so-called 'We passages': 16.10-17; 20.5-16; 21.1-18; 27.1–28.16) indicate that the writer was one of Paul's travelling companions during part of his missionary journeys, and on his last voyage to Rome. We can narrow down the number of possible diarists to a few names like Titus, Jesus Justus, Crescens and Luke.

Third, at this point tradition comes in to help us to a final decision. For the unanimous tradition of the Church in the second century names Luke as the author. There is a strong presumption that the tradition is right. If the book's authorship had been unknown and the Church had been casting about for an author, the odds are that they would have hit on some person of apostolic rank, and not on a comparatively unimportant person like St Luke.

We need only add that odd medical phrases in Luke-Acts (as we may now name the two-volumed work) seem to betray the hand of one whom Paul calls 'the dear doctor' (Col. 4.14).

Concerning Luke himself we have three references in the New Testament (Col. 4.14; Philem. 24; and II Tim. 4.11); a number of traditions, the likeliest of which is

4

that he was a native of Antioch in Syria; and a few guesses, for example, that he is 'the brother whose praise in the Gospel is spread through all the churches' (II Cor. 8.18). What is certain is that he was a Gentile by birth, a physician by profession, a Christian by conversion, and a friend of Paul's by choice. For the rest, if we ask what manner of man he was, the answer is: 'By his books ye shall know him.'

How, why, and when Luke composed his Gospel

In the preface to his Gospel Luke declares: 'Inasmuch as a number of writers have essayed to draw up a narrative of the established facts in our religion, and inasmuch as I have gone carefully over them all myself from the beginning, I have decided, O Theophilus, to write them out in order for your excellency, to let you know the solid truth of what you have been taught' (Moffatt). Here, Luke expressly claims to have 'gone into the sources' (as we should say) and, with our Synoptic studies behind us, we can make a fair guess at them:

Mark.

Q.

L: This source which contains about half of the total bulk of Luke, and comprises many of the finest parables and stories in the Gospels, is probably material which Luke gathered in Caesarea and neighbourhood during the years 57–59. Most of it is in the section 9.51–18.14.

B.S. i.e. Birth Stories (1–2): This material is certainly Palestinian in origin. Many scholars believe that here Luke is employing a source which was originally in Hebrew.

Here is the story which many scholars believe lies behind the writing of the Third Gospel. During that sojourn in Caesarea the idea first occurred to Luke. So much new and precious Gospel tradition had come his way that he conceived the idea of writing a Gospel. At Antioch probably he found Q, and at once started to combine his own material with it into a connected narrative. Then one day lighting on Mark—which had begun to circulate in the Church—he made extracts from it, and fitted them into his first draft ('Proto-Luke', as Streeter calls it). Finally, he added the Birth stories as an introduction and wrote a brief preface.

We do not know precisely when the Gospel first appeared in its complete form. It must have been after A.D. 70; for Luke's language in 21.20 suggests that the siege of Jerusalem was already a past event. On the other hand, it must have been written before the Fourth Gospel which seems to imply knowledge of it. A date about 80 is likely.

If we ask why Luke wrote his Gospel, the probable answer is that he desired to let Theophilus (a high Roman official), and his like, know the 'solid truth' of the religion which they had embraced. Perhaps Luke felt that men like Theophilus needed a 'life' of Christ which would appeal more to their cultivated taste than the roughly written Mark, and one which would make it clearer than Mark does, that Jesus Christ was not only the Messiah of the Jews but the Saviour of all men.

The Contents and Characteristics of the Third Gospel

The Gospel falls into five parts:

(1) The Beginnings (chs. 1–2).

(2) The Call of Jesus (ch. 3–4.13).
(3) The Galilean Ministry (4.14–9.50).
(4) On the Road to Jerusalem (9.51–19.48).
(5) Jerusalem: Crucifixion and Resurrection (chs. 20–24).

If St Mark is 'one of those people who simply cannot tell a story badly', St Luke is one who can tell a story to perfection. This is by far the best written of the Gospels, and the beauty of Luke's style 'survives translation'. Alike in narrative (see the stories of the woman who was a sinner, and the walk to Emmaus) and in pen-portraiture (see the sketches of Zacharias or Zaccheus), we detect the hand of the master. He has dramatic power; he has pathos; and to both he adds that economy of touch—that 'sweet austerity of art'—which we call classical.

When we turn to the contents of the Gospel, our first judgment must be that it is the Gospel for the Gentiles. The Jesus of this Gospel is not primarily the Messiah of the Jews but 'the catholic Christ'. It is no accident that Luke traces Jesus' ancestry back not to Abraham but to Adam. In the song of Simeon Jesus is hailed as 'a light to lighten the Gentiles'. Samaritans are twice singled out by Jesus for high praise. A Gentile centurion is credited with such faith as He had not found in Israel. And the Gospel ends with the command that the Good News be preached to 'all the nations'.

It is the Gospel of 'the underdog'. In no other Gospel do we find such shining and tender emphasis set upon Jesus as 'the friend of publicans and sinners', come 'to seek and to save that which was lost', be it a fallen woman, a despised tax-collector, or a penitent thief. No other evangelist has drawn our Lord's sympathy with

the outcast and the poor with a more gracious pencil;
and together with this sympathy we find grim warning
for the loveless rich—a warning heard first in Mary's
song—

> 'He hath filled the hungry with good things;
> And the rich he hath sent empty away—'

echoed in the Beatitudes ('Blessed are ye poor') and re-
echoed in the parables of the rich fool, and Dives and
Lazarus.

It is the Gospel of womanhood. St Luke delights to
dwell on Christ's tenderness to women. This reverence
for womanhood shines out in the opening idylls of
Elisabeth, Mary and Anna; we find it in the stories of
the woman who was a sinner, of the widow of Nain,
and of Martha and Mary; and it reappears even at the
end in Jesus' words of warning and consolation to 'the
daughters of Jerusalem'.

It is the Gospel of prayer. Here oftener than in any
other we see 'the kneeling Christ', praying before His
Baptism, praying in the solitary places, praying at
Caesarea Philippi, and on the Mount of Transfiguration, praying in the Garden and on the Cross. It is
in this Gospel alone that we find the three parables
of prayer which we know as the Pharisee and the
Publican, the Friend at Midnight and the Importunate
widow.

Lastly, it is the Gospel of joy. There is gladness at its
beginning—'Behold I bring you good tidings of great
joy'—there is gladness in its middle (Chap. 15); and
there is gladness at its ending when the disciples 'returned to Jerusalem with great joy'. 'What a note of
joy, courage and triumph', says Harnack, 'sounds

through the whole Lucan history from the first to the last pages. *Vexilla Regis prodeunt!*"[1]

.It is small wonder that this is the favourite Gospel of many. 'This is the kind of book which brings health to the soul in an age like ours. Its author is still a physician, and still beloved.'[2] The words on the memorial tablet of one Henry Blackstone, in New College Chapel, Oxford, might equally have been written of St Luke: *Et animae et corporis simul medicus* ('Physician alike of soul and body').

[1] *Luke the Physician*, p. 163 n.
[2] A. C. Deane, *How to Understand the Gospels*, p. 87.

VIII

The Jewish Christian Gospel

It was a true instinct that put the Gospel according to St Matthew first in the New Testament. This Gospel with its repeated insistence that Christ came to fulfil the olden prophecies, serves to remind us that 'it is one purpose of God which is being fulfilled throughout both Testaments, one People of God, the story of which is being told from Abel to the apostolic age'. If sometimes we find 'Matthew's' arguments from prophecy 'more ingenious than ingenuous',[1] we do well to remember that through them all he is hammering out one main thesis—that Christianity is not an accident but a consummation, the consummation of God's saving purpose for His People begun in the Old Testament dispensation. Nor would his arguments from prophecy leave his first readers so 'cold' as they sometimes leave us; for both tradition and the contents of his book make it plain that 'Matthew' was a Jewish Christian writing for his fellow-countrymen; and his Gospel is as surely the Gospel for the Jews, as St Luke's is the Gospel for the Gentiles.

Who wrote it, when and where

We have printed the name 'Matthew' in inverted commas. The explanation is simple: modern scholars,

[1] See e.g. Matt. 2.15, 17, 23. Matt. 2.15 (=Hos. 11.1), 'Out of Egypt have I called my son', originally referred to the deliverance of *the people of Israel* from Egypt as described in Exodus.

while they find reason to connect this Gospel with the Apostle Matthew, do not believe, as the early Church did, that he wrote it. We need not go into the matter at length. Enough to say that scholars find it incredible (among other things) that one of the Twelve could have copied so closely, as 'Matthew' does, the work of Mark who was not one of the Twelve. (606 of Mark's 661 verses are found in Matthew.) Why then did the early Church so consistently associate the Apostle Matthew's name with the first Gospel that we know it to-day as St Matthew? Our discussion of the Synoptic problem has already supplied the answer: because it is probable that the Apostle Matthew was one of the contributors to the Gospel—in other words, he compiled Q which is one of the Gospel's main sources.

The name of the first evangelist eludes us, but a study of his work 'bewrays' him for the man he was: a Greek-speaking Jewish Christian with something of the Law still clinging to him—or to borrow words from his own book: 'a scribe discipled to the Kingdom of Heaven'. (The very phrase 'Kingdom of Heaven' which he uses in preference to 'the Kingdom of God' reveals the good Jew's avoidance of the divine name.)

Since he used Mark, and since a verse like 22.7 suggests that Jerusalem had already fallen, he must have written after 70. But he must have written before 96; for Clement of Rome apparently knew his Gospel. Perhaps 85 is the best date for his work. If we ask where he wrote, Antioch seems to have the strongest claim. Ignatius of Antioch early in the second century refers to Matthew as 'the Gospel', and the tone of the book is entirely consonant with such a place of origin.

The Sources 'Matthew' used

What sources did 'Matthew' use and how did he use them? To answer briefly, he used three sources—Mark, Q, and M (this symbol standing for all the matter peculiar to Matthew),[1] and he so used them as to produce 'a revised and enlarged edition of Mark'.

'Matthew' *revised* Mark in three ways: first, by improving his rough style; second, by shortening his narrative; third, by rearranging his order in some places.

Likewise, he *enlarged* Mark in three ways: first, by adding narrative matter at the beginning and end of the story (viz. the Birth stories, and extra incidents in the Passion story); second, by incorporating five great discourses; third, by inserting eleven Old Testament proof texts, or testimonies.

But Mark was his framework, and into it he fitted the new materials from Q and M, joining like to like (e.g. Matt. 13 which is based on Mark 4, contains also material from Q and M besides a 'testimony').

'Special Matthew', or M, comprises both narrative and teaching. Of the latter we may instance Matt. 6.1–18; also several valuable parables such as the unmerciful servant, the labourers in the vineyard, the two sons and the ten virgins. The narrative peculiar to Matthew includes stories about Peter and Pilate, and incidents like the coin in the fish's mouth, and the sealing of the Tomb. Here, it must be frankly admitted, we have the least valuable stratum (historically) in the Synoptic Gospels; and for the purpose of reconstructing the story of Jesus we may safely discard it.

---

[1] Streeter uses this symbol to denote a Jerusalem sayings-source which he believes 'Matthew' to have drawn on for his account of Jesus' teaching. We use it generally to denote material peculiar to Matthew.

The Contents and Characteristics of the First Gospel

Since 'Matthew's' account of Jesus' ministry is based
on Mark, a short synopsis of contents is all that is
needed now:

(1) The Nativity (chs. 1–2).
(2) Preparation for the Ministry (ch. 3–4.11).
(3) The Galilean Ministry (4.12–15.20).
(4) Ministry in the neighbourhood of Galilee (15.21–
    18.35).
(5) Journey to Jerusalem (ch. 19–20.34).
(6) The Last Week in Jerusalem (ch. 21–28.10).
(7) The Appearance of the Risen Lord (28.11-20).

Though Matthew has borrowed so much from Mark,
he has passed the material through his own mint and
put his own individual stamp on his work. Someone has
summed up these special Matthaean features in a little
rhyme:

> 'Matthew gives us five discourses;
> In threes and sevens he likes his sources;
> He writes to show what O.T. meant,
> With an ecclesiastic bent.'

'Matthew gives us five discourses':

The Sermon on the Mount (chs. 5–7).
The Charge to the Twelve (ch. 10).
The Parables of the Kingdom (ch. 13).
On true greatness and forgiveness (ch. 18).
On the Last Things (chs. 24–25).

These five discourses, each ending with the refrain 'And
it came to pass when Jesus had ended these words',
reveal 'Matthew's' most striking characteristic: his love

of systematic grouping of Jesus' sayings. We may guess
that he had the needs of catechumens in view, and
wished to present 'the new Law' of Christ in a simple
and memorable form. Since it is 'Matthew's' way thus
to gather Jesus' sayings into great bouquets (like some
gardener with varied flowers), we must not look for
chronological order in his record of Christ's teaching;
for him 'the words that will never pass away have
already shaken off the manacles of time'.[1]

'In threes and sevens he likes his sources':

This second characteristic appears even in the
genealogy of Jesus which opens the Gospel. It falls into
three groups of fourteen names (2×7); and possibly the
whole thing is an acrostic on the name of David whose
letters in Hebrew add up to fourteen. We notice also
that there are three angelic messages to Joseph, three
denials by Peter, three questions by Pilate, as there are
seven parables in Chap. 13, and seven woes in Chap. 23.

'He writes to show what O.T. meant':

that is, he sets out to prove that Jesus Christ is 'Yea
and Amen' to all the promises of God made under the
old dispensation. Jesus 'came not to destroy but to fulfil
the Law and the Prophets' (that is, Old Testament
religion). No less than eight times is Jesus hailed as 'the
Son of David'. In fine, where Mark shows us the strong
Son of God, and Luke the catholic Christ, Matthew
shows us Him 'who appeared in the fullness of time, in
whose life the word of Psalmists and Prophets found
their fulfilment, who was the Messiah of whom Jewish

[1] Levertoff and Goudge in Gore's *New Commentary on Holy
Scripture*, St Matthew, p. 127.

history had been one long prophecy, who came to fulfil the old Law by making it new, who was born king and lawgiver of the new *ecclesia* which was the true People of God'.[1]

'With an ecclesiastic bent':

We have already noted 'Matthew's' tendency to systematize with the needs of the young *ecclesia* in view. He alone among the evangelists uses the word 'church' (16.18; 18.17). He alone inserts 'the excepting clause'[2] into Christ's saying about the sanctity of marriage (5.32; 19.9). And it is to him that we owe the Trinitarian Baptismal formula (28.19).

As a 'life' of Christ we must account Matthew the least valuable of the Synoptic Gospels; but as a repository of Christ's teaching it has been, and always will be, highly prized. Nor can we ever think without affection of the evangelist who begins his story with the birth of Him who is 'Immanuel—God with us' and whose final word is, 'Lo, I am with you alway, even unto the end of the world.'

[1] Clogg: *Introduction to the New Testament*, p. 225 f.
[2] 'Saving for the cause of fornication.' It probably represents not the mind of Christ, but the practice of some part of the early Christian Church. Cf. Mark 10.11–12; Luke 16.18.

IX

The Spiritual Gospel

A FEW years ago there was unearthed from the sands of
Egypt a tiny bit of papyrus with some thirty Greek
words written on it. When the experts had examined it,
they pronounced it a piece of the New Testament which
must have been written about A.D. 130. It is the earliest
piece of the New Testament extant, and now reposes in
the Rylands Library, Manchester.

This fragment is, in fact, a tiny bit of the Gospel
according to St John, the Fourth Gospel, or, as a famous
Father of the Early Church (Clement of Alexandria)
called it, 'The Spiritual Gospel.' (It contains John 18.31-
33, 37-38.)

The Author of the Fourth Gospel

Who was the Fourth Evangelist?

From the second century onwards it was generally
believed that the author was the Apostle John, the
brother of James and son of Zebedee, who, according
to tradition, lived to a ripe old age in Ephesus. Thus
Irenaeus, about A.D. 180, could write: 'John the disciple
of the Lord who also leaned on his breast, himself too
set forth the Gospel while dwelling in Ephesus.' (Some
late and dubious evidence that John the Apostle was
martyred may be discounted.) In support of the tradition of apostolic authorship two considerations can be
advanced: (1) The Gospel and First Epistle of John
both claim to depend on an eyewitness (John 1.14;
19.35; I John 1.1-4). This witness is called in the Gospel
'the disciple whom Jesus loved' (13.23; 19.26; 20.2 ff.;

21.7, 20); and if we ask who he was, the obvious and simple answer is: John the Apostle who is never mentioned by name in the Gospel. (2) A study of the Gospel shows the author to have been remarkably 'well-up' in the geography of the Holy Land, particularly of Jerusalem, while his style suggests a man whose mother-tongue was Aramaic.

Certain other considerations, however, bid us pause before accepting the verdict of tradition. Thus (1) we must think it improbable that one of the Twelve would have used the work of Mark and Luke who were not of that blessed number, as the Fourth Evangelist apparently did.[1] (2) There is the matter of style. Jesus in the Synoptic Gospels speaks one way—with a wealth of parables, and in short, pithy, vivid sentences—in St John, in quite another: for here there are no parables, but long mystical discourses whose style often closely resembles that of the evangelist himself. (3) We must judge it psychologically unlikely that the Apostle John would have styled himself 'the disciple whom Jesus loved'. For these and other reasons, scarcely a reputable scholar in this country nowadays is prepared to affirm that the Fourth Gospel was written by John the Apostle.

On the other hand, the book shows so intimate a knowledge of the Holy Land, contains so many tokens of an eyewitness, has so clear a note of apostolic authority that we may agree with Dr Temple: 'I regard as self-condemned any theory of authorship which fails to find a very close connexion between the Gospel and the son of Zebedee.'[2]

What then? The simplest and most satisfying solution

---

[1] See Streeter, *The Four Gospels*, Chap. xiv.
[2] *Readings in St John's Gospel*, p. x.

of the problem is that which discovers in the author a devoted disciple of the Apostle John. Who could this be? In the second and third Epistles of John[1] the writer calls himself 'the Elder' (II John 1; III John 1). Now Papias refers to *two* Johns in the early Church: one, a disciple of the Lord, apparently deceased (the Apostle John?); and the other still living whom he calls 'the Elder John', while there is some evidence connecting this John with Ephesus (a fourth-century document names as bishops of Ephesus 'Timothy ordained by Paul and John by John'). If we find the author of the Gospel in this 'Elder John', we can understand how he might be confused with the Apostle John in the early tradition. Our conclusion then is that if we are to put a name on the title page of the Fourth Gospel, there is no better candidate in the field than John the Elder, and we may neatly describe the Fourth Gospel as, 'The Gospel of John (the Elder) according to John (the Son of Zebedee).'

As to place of writing, tradition is all in favour of Ephesus and we may well accept it. The date of writing was probably in the last decade of the first century.

The Contents of the Gospel

It is usual to begin by emphasizing the differences between the Fourth Gospel and the Synoptic Gospels: to point out that in the selection of incidents, the scene of Christ's ministry, the form and substance of His teaching, and chronology, the Gospel according to St John presents a decisive contrast to the first three. That these differences exist, we are not concerned to deny. Though John re-tells some of the Synoptic stories, he

[1] These, with the First Epistle of John, are generally supposed to be by the same author.

does break new ground elsewhere. According to him, Jerusalem saw a great deal more of Christ during His ministry than the Synoptists (on the surface at least) suggest. He does, as we have already noted, make Christ speak differently from the Christ of the Synoptics. He does differ from the Synoptists in matters of chronology; for example, he puts the cleansing of the Temple at the beginning of the ministry, and the crucifixion a day earlier than the Synoptists—on the day of the killing of the Passover Lamb, and not the day after, as in the Synoptics. Yet it is easy to exaggerate these differences; for the Synoptists (to take only one or two points) do throw out hints that Christ was oftener in Jerusalem than their story records; and when once we have grasped that there is no essential difference between 'the Kingdom of God'—which is Jesus' main theme in the Synoptics—and 'eternal life'—which is His main theme in the Fourth Gospel—the alleged difference in teaching does not appear so serious. But—to speak generally—it must be insisted that in broad outline John tells the same story as Mark had told thirty years earlier: how Jesus was baptized in Jordan, how He called disciples and went through Galilee and Judea announcing the advent of God's salvation; how enemies arose against Him; and how at last He was arrested, condemned and crucified. And there follows the same astounding sequel of the empty grave and the risen Lord.

But John does not simply repeat the same sequence of events. Some of the most familiar incidents in Christ's life—like the Baptism, the Temptation, the Transfiguration, the Agony in the Garden, and the institution of the Lord's Supper—he leaves out. On the other hand, he tells new stories about Jesus: how He talked with Nicodemus; or with the woman by Jacob's well; how He raised Lazarus from the dead; how, on the last night, He washed the disciples' feet; and how, after the resurrection, He appeared first to Mary Magdalene in the Garden, then to doubting Thomas in the upper room, and last of all, to seven disciples by the Lake in the grey of a Galilean dawn.

Yet, if John's outline is broadly the same, he tells the story with a difference—a difference of style, of atmosphere, and of treatment.

Let us pick out three examples:

First, John opens differently. Matthew and Luke begin with Jesus' birth in Bethlehem, as Mark begins at Jordan. But John who sees the whole story of Jesus in the light of eternity, begins it in heaven. 'In the beginning was the Word,' he begins superbly, 'and the Word was with God, and the Word was God.' A word is an uttered thought. The Word of God is His thought uttered so that men may understand it. It was by the Word of God, says John, that all things were made; that is to say, all creation is a revelation of the thought of God. All down the ages God has been uttering His thought—His Word—but when the fullness of the time was come, God clothed His thought in flesh and blood —in terms of a human life. 'The Word became flesh and dwelt among us':

> 'And so the Word had breath; and wrought
> With human hands the creed of creeds.
> In loveliness of perfect deeds
> More strong than all poetic thought.'[1]

Now for a second difference. The first three Gospels all record that Jesus wrought mighty works and

[1] Tennyson.

5

miracles. So does John: he records seven, but he calls them by a different name: 'signs', i.e. symbols of a deeper truth: indications of who and what Jesus is. He is always at pains to bring out this deeper meaning. Thus, John tells us how Jesus fed the multitude at what we called 'the Galilean Lord's Supper'. But he immediately follows it with a discourse by Jesus about the Bread of Life. This meaning *may* be implicit in the story as Mark tells it; John makes it fully explicit. Or, again, he relates how Jesus raised Lazarus from the dead, but at the same time records how Jesus claimed to be the giver of eternal life alike to living and dead: 'I am the resurrection and the life.'

Perhaps the most striking difference lies in John's record of what passed between Jesus and the disciples on the night of the Last Supper. If we had only the first three Gospels, we should know little beyond the fact that they held the Last Supper together. But John in chapters 13–17 lifts the veil, and lets us peer into the Holy of Holies—lets us hear Jesus speaking with His own on that night never to be effaced from memory. Each chapter is pure gold; but if we single out the fourteenth chapter: 'Let not your heart be troubled'; the fifteenth, 'I am the true vine'; and the seventeenth which contains Jesus' great prayer for His disciples, we have named those which, all down the centuries, have nourished the faith and life of Christian people. In the whole library of Holy Writ there is nothing more sublime.

The Value of the Gospel

What is the special virtue and value of the Fourth Gospel? In his poem, 'A Death in the Desert', Brown-

ing imaginatively reconstructs the last hours of the
Apostle John and sets these words upon his lips:

> 'What first were guessed as points I now knew stars
> And named them in the Gospel I have writ.'

Nothing could better suggest the special contribution of
John to the Gospel story. He it was who, by virtue of
his long and deep Christian experience, was enabled to
take the Gospel 'points' and to set them forth in all
their starry splendour. Point after point he lights up
with heavenly meaning. But consider the figure of Jesus
Himself. In our churches the stained-glass windows
often depict scenes from the ministry of Jesus, showing
Him as teacher, friend, or lover of little children. Now
you may spend hours wholly absorbed in the details;
but there is always the danger that you may not see the
wood for trees. Sometimes, however, the artist has decided that you shall not miss the central meaning; so,
high up in the central light, he has painted Christ in
glory holding, it may be, an orb of the world in His
hand. When you step back from the window to see it
properly, the figure of Christ dominates everything, and
all the details serve to show forth His glory. John did
something very like this in his Gospel. You may read
Mark, and Luke, and get so engrossed in the details
about the man Jesus that you fail to see the divine halo
around His head. But John knew that the Jesus who
had once lived and died in Galilee was now 'the Lord
of glory'. So he resolved to show us Christ in His true
nature and setting—the divine Christ who came forth
from the bosom of the Father, unveiled Him to men,
died for the world's sin, rose again and passed to the
right hand of God, whence He comes again through His

Spirit[1] to those who love Him. In short, he shows us Jesus not as a figure of ancient history but as the eternal contemporary, the light of the world, the only true and living way, now as then, to God:

> 'For in him was hid the secret
> That through all ages ran.'

And he sums up the message of the Gospel for all time in one great, golden sentence: 'God so loved the world that he gave his only begotten Son that whosoever believeth on him should not perish but have eternal life' (3.16).

No book in the whole Bible has influenced the faith and life of Christians like this one.[2] Simple peasants have read it and had their faith deepened and confirmed. Learned scholars have brooded over it and found its riches inexhaustible. 'I meditate on St John's Gospel,' said Wordsworth, 'and my creed rises with the ease of an exhalation.' And many will recall how Sir Walter Scott on his death-bed made Lockhart read to him from this Gospel; and, when the reading was over, confessed, 'Well, this is a great comfort.' As long as the world lasts, men will turn to 'the spiritual Gospel' for light in darkness and comfort in despair; nor will they be disappointed.

'To the pilgrim seeking the way that leads to truth and peace the evangelist brings his message that he who

---

[1] See John 14.15-17, 25-26; 15.26-27; 16.5-11, 12-15. John's name for the Holy Spirit is 'the Paraclete', i.e. 'Helper'. His purpose, according to St John, is not so much to supply Christ's absence as to *accomplish His presence*.

[2] As Sir E. Hoskyns says in his commentary on the Fourth Gospel, p. 6, more than any other this Gospel has been 'the textbook of the parish-priest and the inspiration of the straightforward layman'.

follows Jesus shall not walk in darkness but shall have
the light of life. To those who long for the assurance of
eternal life there is given also the open secret, "Because
I live, ye shall live also." But the final word of the Gospel is that only "those who love will ever understand".
To-day, as nineteen hundred years ago, the disciple who
loves his Lord and is loved by Him will discern His
face through the morning mist. And now as in the days
of old beside the Galilean lake, the ardent defender of
the cause of Christ is still met with the thrice-repeated
challenge: "Lovest thou me?".[1]

Note

Two technical points deserve mention in a note. (1)
John 7.53–8.11, the story of the woman taken in adul-
tery, though a genuine piece of tradition, is no real part
of this Gospel. The story is absent from our oldest
manuscripts; its style resembles the Synoptic Gospels,
and indeed it is found in some manuscripts attached to
Luke 21.37. (2) Chapter 21 reads like an Appendix
added to the Gospel at a later date; for it looks as
though the Gospel originally ended at 20.30 f., but a
study of its style suggests that it comes from the same
hand as the rest of the Gospel. It was probably added
to clear up a misunderstanding about 'the beloved disciple' (see any good commentary).

[1] W. F. Howard, *The Fourth Gospel in Recent Criticism and Interpretation*, p. 244.

PART THREE

THE EARLY CHURCH AND ST PAUL

X

How They Brought the Good News from Jerusalem to Rome

EVERY schoolboy knows Browning's poem, 'How They Brought the Good News from Ghent to Aix', with its electric beginning:

> 'I sprang to the stirrup, and Joris, and he;
> I galloped, Dirck galloped, we galloped all three.'

If you change the two place-names and for Ghent and Aix write Jerusalem and Rome, you get an admirable description of the book we know as 'The Acts of the Apostles'. It is the story of how they—the apostles of Christ—brought the Good News of the Gospel from Jerusalem to Rome; from the Holy City to the capital of the world. And the story, though much longer than Browning's, is no less stirring, if we read it with a little historical imagination. For the Acts of the Apostles is, as the title suggests, full of action and adventure; of plots and daring escapes; of earthquakes and ship-wrecks; of trials and prisons and riots and victories; with all the sights and sounds and colours of the Middle East in the first century of our era. 'A book from the ancient East, and lit up by the light of the dawn—a book breathing the fragrance of the Galilean spring, and anon swept by the shipwrecking north-east tempest from the Mediterranean—a book of peasants, fishermen, artisans, travellers by land and sea, fighters and martyrs—a book in cosmopolitan Greek with marks of Semitic origin—a book of the Imperial age, written at Antioch, Ephesus, Corinth, Rome—a book of pictures, miracles and visions—book of the village and the town —book of the people and the peoples'—these fine words of Deissmann,[1] though he writes of the New Testament as a whole, apply with singular fitness to the Acts of the Apostles.

The Author and his Book

We do not need to spend time discussing who the author was. The man who wrote the Acts was the same man who wrote the Third Gospel, Luke the beloved physician; and Acts, as we saw already, is really the second volume of his work on 'The Beginnings of Christianity'. Volume I had recounted 'all that Jesus began to do and to teach'. But Jesus had promised, 'The works that I do shall ye do also,' and in Volume II Luke shows us how that promise came true—how the apostles, inspired by the Spirit, brought the Good News about Jesus from Jerusalem through Samaria and Syria and over the blue waters of the Mediterranean via Greece to Rome.

We have seen already that Luke dedicates both his books to 'your excellency', Theophilus, who was probably a Gentile of high official rank. (Our equivalent of 'your excellency' would be 'Right Honourable'). Theophilus was no doubt typical of the audience for whom Luke designed his work. Luke wrote to give such men a full account of the beginnings of the new religion and to commend it to them. The last clause perhaps needs

[1] *Light from the Ancient East*, p. 392.

to be underlined. A study of Luke-Acts makes it fairly clear that Luke was concerned to vindicate Christianity in the eyes of his Gentile readers—to convince them that Christianity presented no threat to the government of the Roman Empire, as its enemies wickedly insinuated. That is why in Luke-Acts there is a consistent tendency to acquit the Roman authorities of blame in their treatment first of Jesus and later of Paul, and to saddle the Jews with the chief responsibility. (Thus, to take one example only, 'three times over, it is shown, first Jesus and then Paul are pronounced not guilty of civil misdemeanour, Jesus three times by Pilate (Luke 23.4, 14, 22), Paul by Gallio, Festus and Agrippa' (Acts 18.14; 26.31 f.).)

We have Luke's own word for it that when he was writing his Gospel he made a serious attempt to 'go into the sources'; and there is no doubt that in writing Acts he did the same. But it is not so easy to define his sources here. In the second part of Acts (16–28), which deals with the doings of St Paul, we need have no doubt about his sources of information. Here he had his own travel-diary of which the 'we passages' are samples, and, of course, he had Paul himself for informant. But in the first half of his narrative he is telling the story of events which happened long before he came personally on the scene; and we can only speculate about his sources. If he tells us about the mother-Church in Jerusalem in its earliest days we must suppose that John Mark or Peter was his informant.[1] For his knowledge of the Church in Caesarea, we may safely guess that Philip, who lived there, and with whom Paul and Luke 'stayed many days' (Acts 21.10), was his authority.[2] And as for the

[1] e.g. for most of chaps. 1–5.   [2] e.g. chap. 10.

Church in Antioch, of which he gives a full account,[1] we know that he visited Antioch and met the brethren there, and it is possible, even probable, that Luke was himself a native of that city.

Concerning the date of the Acts there is still much dispute. An early date (about 64) seems excluded by the fact that Luke used Mark in composing his Gospel, and Acts comes later. Besides, the Gospel seems in one passage (21.20) to reflect the Fall of Jerusalem. On the other hand, those who date the book very late (about 95) assume that Luke had read—or rather misread—a work of Josephus, the Jewish historian, written about 93. This is not proven. On the whole, it seems best to date the Acts a few years after the Gospel, that is, about A.D. 85.

With this brief discussion of technicalities, let us turn now to the book itself.

The Contents of Acts

The Book of Acts contains twenty-eight chapters, and these describe a period of (roughly) thirty years—A.D. 30–60.

We may conveniently divide the book into two parts.

Part I consists of chapters 1–12, and tells how Peter and the first Christians brought the Gospel from Jerusalem to Antioch in Syria. Here, after an opening chapter which describes Jesus' leave-taking of His disciples and the election of a man, Matthias, to fill Judas' place, we get glimpses of the mother-Church in Jerusalem on the day of Pentecost, when the promised Spirit came upon the waiting Church, and of the spread of the Faith in and around Jerusalem. Under the impulsion of the

[1] 11.19–30.

Spirit the Church grows apace, with Peter as its acknow-
ledged leader. At first there is no breach with Jewry,
but by and by the new wine begins to burst the old
wineskins. Stephen, the first to grasp the essential newness of the Faith, by his bold speech calls down the ire
of the Jews upon himself, and is stoned to death.
Persecution at once breaks out, and with the consequent
dispersal of the Church the circle of the Gospel's influence widens; the 'hallowed fire' spreads, through
Philip, to Samaria, and from Samaria down to the sea-
coast at Caesarea, and finally to Syrian Antioch, the
third city of the Roman Empire, and the place where
the noble name of Christian was first coined.

Part II consists of chapters 13–28. If Peter was the
leading figure in Part I, now it is Paul (of whose conversion we have heard in Part I) who gradually ad-
vances to the centre of the stage; so that we may call
Part II, 'How Paul and his friends carried the Gospel
from Antioch to Rome.' First we see Paul and Barnabas
set out on their first missionary journey from Antioch
to the island of Cyprus (Barnabas' native soil), and
then to Galatia in Asia Minor. After that follows the
first Council of the Church in Jerusalem to decide on
what terms Gentiles are to be admitted into the Christian fellowship: an issue precipitated by the missionary
success of Paul and Barnabas. Then Paul and Silas
make a second missionary journey in the course of
which, after traversing Asia Minor, they bring the Gospel to the shores of Europe; and in Macedonia, Athens
and Corinth the Faith is proclaimed.

Paul's third missionary journey sees the Gospel firmly
planted in the great heathen city of Ephesus before Paul
once again sets foot in Europe.

Then Luke's history moves to its climax. Returning to Jerusalem Paul is attacked by the Jews, and put under arrest by the Romans. As a Roman citizen he appeals to Caesar for justice. For two years he lies in prison at Caesarea; then he is taken by sea to Rome, being shipwrecked, *en route*, on Malta; and the book ends with Paul still a prisoner—in a sort of free custody —awaiting the Emperor's verdict. '*Paulus Romae, apex evangelii, Actorum finis*,' says the old commentator, Bengel: 'Paul in Rome, the climax of the Gospel; the end of Acts.'

But it is rather an abrupt ending. Why did not Luke tell us what happened to St Paul? The abrupt ending and the fact that in Acts 1.1 Luke calls his Gospel, literally, 'the *first* treatise' (AV and RV 'former') have led some scholars to suppose that Luke contemplated a third volume in which the story of Paul's end would have been told. That Luke projected a three-volumed work, a trilogy, is very possible; but more than that we cannot say.

The Value of Acts

The first question we ask of any historian's work is: Is his history in substantial accord with the facts so far as we can judge? Does he tell a reliable story? Judged by this test the book of Acts must be accounted good history. There was a time when Luke's credit as a historian did not stand so high as it does now. A famous school of German scholarship decided that in Acts we had an *eirēnikon*—a document that deliberately set out to gloss over the divergencies in the early Church between Peter and Paul by turning a Nelson eye on them. Nowadays there are not many to be found supporting this view. It is true that there are still some apparent discrepancies between the book of Acts and the Pauline epistles, but few that cannot either be reconciled or satisfactorily explained. Thanks to the archaeological labours of Sir William Ramsay and others we know now that the book is not a historical romance, or a book of legends, or a third-rate chronicle, but a first-rate history in which 'the narrative shows marvellous truth', not only in its broad outlines but even in the smallest details —like the titles of the local magistrates in Thessalonica ('politarchs'), or the Mediterranean harbours, or the customs and legends current in various places like Lystra. Naturally, as history, the second half of Acts, where Luke is writing with first-hand knowledge of the facts, stands higher than the first; but even in the first half we have no reason to believe that the broad picture Luke paints of the early Church is untrue. Even the speeches of Peter and others which used to be dismissed as free compositions of St Luke, are now seen to enshrine early Christian tradition. Verbatim reports they are not; but if a speech such as Acts 10.34-43 does not transcribe the very words of Peter, it must represent the general burden of his preaching.

The second question we ask of a historian is: Can he tell his story well? Judged by this test, Luke can hold his own with almost any historian, ancient or modern. His book is full of grand stories, superbly told: the martyrdom of Stephen (6-7); the escape of Peter from prison (12); Paul and Silas in the gaol at Philippi (16); the riot in the theatre at Ephesus (19); and the storm and shipwreck on the voyage to Rome (27). In scene after scene we watch the Gospel going forward victoriously against all the forces of paganism: sorcery,

magic, superstition, immorality, blind bigotry and preju-
dice. And with what splendid figures Luke crowds his
pages: Stephen the first martyr; Peter now more like a
'rock' than when his Master first gave him the name;
James now a staunch believer in his divine Brother;
Apollos the eloquent man from Alexandria; Priscilla
and Aquila, that fine Christian couple; good-hearted
Barnabas; Paul the dauntless, and many another. And
besides these apostolic men what a varied collection of
notable pagans who in one way or another came within
the orbit of the advancing Gospel: Gamaliel, the sage
rabbi, at whose feet Paul had once sat; Simon the
sorcerer; the effete intellectuals of Athens who dubbed
Paul 'the little cocksparrow'; Demetrius, the Ephesian
silversmith, with his fellow trade-unionists; the Roman
consul Gallio who 'turned his dainty nose away lest the
breath of the Ghetto should come between the wind and
his nobility'.[1]

But perhaps the chief merit of Acts for the simple
believer is that it forms a valuable bridge between the
days of Christ's flesh and ourselves. There are some
who suppose that belief in the Gospel is harder for us
than for those who knew Christ as a man in Galilee.
Ah, if only they had been living 'in that great day'. . . .

'I think when I read that sweet story of old
    When Jesus was here among men,
How He called little children as lambs to His fold,
    I should like to have been with them then.'

But this wistful longing for a figure in past history is
not Christianity. We worship not a dead teacher but a
living Lord. And it is just here that Acts helps us to a

[1] J. A. Findlay, *Acts*, p. 13.

truer view; for in this book we see men and women who, though Christ's bodily presence is no longer with them, know beyond all shadow of doubt that He lives and reigns, and His presence is available for them in 'all the changing scenes of life'.

In Masefield's play, *The Trial of Jesus*, Longinus, the Roman centurion, who stood at the foot of the Cross, is heard talking with Procula, Pilate's wife, just after the crucifixion. 'Do you think he is dead?' she asks him. 'No, lady, I don't.' 'Then where is he?' 'Let loose in the world, lady,' replies Longinus, 'where neither Roman nor Jew can stop his truth.' It is that Christ 'let loose in the world', the Christ who stands by His servants in all their trials and dangers, who is the central figure in the book of Acts, as He is the central figure to-day in the lives of all who seek to follow in the steps of 'the glorious company of the apostles'.

XI

St Paul

OF all the great men of antiquity there is none, Cicero
perhaps excepted, whom we may know better than St
Paul. Not only do we have the story of a large part of
his life written for us by his friend Luke in the Acts; but
we have at least ten of his letters. And such letters!
Paul's letters are intensely alive, his words, as Luther
said, 'hands and feet to carry a man away'. True, we
have not all Paul's letters, and those we have cover a
period of only ten to twelve years (roughly A.D. 50–60).
But with Luke's narrative as framework and the ten
letters, we have enough for a life of Paul.

Saul or Paul (one was his Jewish, the other his Gentile name) was born, probably about the same time as
our Lord, in the city of Tarsus in Cilicia. Tarsus was an
important centre of commerce, a famous university
town, and a meeting place for Hellenism and Oriental-
ism: 'no undistinguished city', as its greatest son once
said. Paul's parents, who were Pharisees (the Puritans of
Judaism), nurtured their son in the straitest tenets of the
Jewish religion. His father, probably a man of some
standing, was a Roman citizen, and his son inherited
that proud privilege. Following the wise Jewish custom
that every lad, whatever calling he contemplated, should
have a trade, Paul learned tent-making—a craft that
was later to serve him well. The other thing worth
noting is that in cosmopolitan Tarsus the young Paul
came into close contact with the Greek world, and his

resultant knowledge of Hellenism was an important element in the training of one who was to be 'the Apostle to the Gentiles'.

Paul's parents had evidently set their heart on their son becoming a 'doctor of the Law'; and about the age of fourteen he must have sailed for Jerusalem to study the Law under Gamaliel, one of the greatest rabbis of all time. All our information proclaims Gamaliel a man of liberal and catholic mind, and his teaching must have deeply influenced Paul at this malleable period of his life.

Paul grew to manhood and (as he says) 'advanced in the Jews' religion beyond many of his countrymen'.[1] What destiny awaited him? Was he fated to follow in the footsteps of his great teacher?

Providence had other plans. About the year A.D. 30, a young Nazarene called Jesus was crucified in Jerusalem—perhaps, if II Cor. 5.16 gets its obvious meaning, before the very eyes of Paul. This Jesus had affronted the majesty of the ancient Law, had claimed a knowledge of God that to the Pharisees seemed blasphemous, and by word and deed, towards the end of His career, had suggested that He was the long-looked-for Messiah. But, at last, He had paid the penalty which every such pretender deserved, by dying a death pronounced accursed by the Jewish Law.

But if Paul's set supposed that the crucifixion was the end of the pretender, they were mightily mistaken. A few days later His followers were filling Jerusalem with the news that God has raised Jesus from the dead and made Him 'Lord and Christ'. To Jews like Paul, this was nonsense. Yet the heresy spread, and in a year or

[1] Gal. 1.14.

two the followers of 'The Way' (as they were called) had so multiplied that Paul and his friends grew alarmed. One of the boldest of Jesus' followers, a Greek-speaking Jew named Stephen, even dared to assert that Jesus Christ has superseded the Law and the Temple. This was the last straw. 'They stoned Stephen calling upon the Lord and saying, Lord Jesus receive my spirit . . . and the witnesses laid down their garments at the feet of a young man named Saul.' 'If Stephen had not prayed,' said Augustine, 'the Church would not have had Paul.'

Stephen's death was the signal for a bitter persecution of the Christians in Jerusalem. Most of them fled the city, some going to Damascus, others as far as Antioch in Syria. Paul, resolved that he could best serve God by stamping out this heresy, and armed with a commission from the High Priest for this purpose, set out for Damascus a hundred and fifty miles away. What happened on the road to Damascus is history and need not be rehearsed at length. 'The vision came in the desert where men see visions and hear voices to this day. The Spirit of Jesus, as he came to call it, spoke to his heart and the form of Jesus flashed before his eyes. Stephen had been right. The Crucified was indeed the Lord of heaven.'[1] So Saul became a Christian, or (to use his own phrase) 'a man in Christ'.

No doubt his conversion was, in some sense, the last explosive stage in a long process of inner-search. His haunting sense of failure—failure to win by observance of the Law that peace of mind for which he longed— was one factor in his conversion. No doubt the impression made upon him by the triumphant death of

[1] Dean Inge in *Outspoken Essays* (First Series), p. 218.

Stephen was another. Perhaps his journey to Damascus was a desperate endeavour to stifle his doubts by action. But all attempts to rationalize the actual experience on the Damascus road by calling it, for example, 'a discharging lesion of the occipital cortex, he being an epileptic', utterly fail to explain an experience which transformed Saul the persecutor into Paul the dynamic apostle of Christ. For the experience Paul had himself only one explanation: 'I was arrested by Christ Jesus': 'He appeared to me also.'

Paul was received into the Christian fellowship at Damascus through the agency of Ananias. What followed is not quite clear; but, combining the data of Acts 9 and Gal. 1, we may suppose that he first retired into Arabia—the desert country south of Damascus—to think out the implications of his experience, and perhaps to begin missionary work, before returning to Damascus where he began to preach Jesus as the Messiah. Eventually, Damascus grew too hot for him, and he was forced to make a daring 'get-away' from the city (Acts 9.24; II Cor. 11.32 f.).

So, three years after his conversion, he came again to Jerusalem (Acts 9.26; Gal. 1.18-24). For a fortnight he 'interviewed' Peter and 'we may presume that they did not spend all their time talking about the weather'. Then Paul retired, perhaps on the advice of his friends who feared for his safety, to his native country of Cilicia, and for some ten years—'the hidden years' of Paul's life—he disappears from view. To those ten years must belong many of the adventures listed in II Cor. 11.23-27, as also the mystical experience 'above fourteen years ago' (II Cor. 12.2 ff.).

He reappears in Antioch, the capital of Syria. After

the outbreak of persecution in Jerusalem, Antioch had become the second great Christian centre. Hither the mother-Church had sent Barnabas to report on the Antioch Church, and especially on the conversion of the Gentiles. To him belongs the honour of recalling Paul from Tarsus (Acts 11.25). After working together in Antioch for a year, Barnabas and Paul went to Jerusalem (we assume that the visit recorded in Acts 11.30 is the same as that described in Gal. 2.1 ff.). A famine was threatening Judea, and the two delegates from Antioch took with them a relief contribution for the Jerusalem Church. On this occasion Paul, who was still suspect in many eyes, ventured to submit his Gospel to the 'pillar' apostles in Jerusalem. Not only did they endorse it, but they made an agreement on respective spheres of missionary work: 'We (i.e. Paul and Barnabas) were to go to the Gentiles, and they to the Circumcision' (Gal. 2.9).

The First Journey (*Acts 12–14*)

He started on his first journey with Barnabas and his cousin, John Mark. From Antioch they sailed to Cyprus, of which Barnabas was a native. Then, after a short mission there, they sailed north-west to the coast of Asia Minor where at Perga, John Mark, for some reason (homesickness? funk?) left them in the lurch. Moving inland to Antioch in Pisidia, they began work in the local synagogue. (This was Paul's usual plan of campaign: he would begin in the synagogue which generally had an outer circle of Gentile adherents; then, when Jewish hostility forced him to leave, he would take with him the nucleus of a small Christian community.) They continued to preach till Jewish antipathy expelled them from the district; then they moved on along the Roman road to Iconium, Lystra and Derbe in the south of the Roman province of Galatia. Here much the same sequence of events was repeated, though at Lystra the people began by attempting to worship Barnabas and Paul, and ended by stoning Paul. Then, turning back, they secured the Christian conquests already made, and returned by sea to Syrian Antioch, only to learn that a crisis was brewing in the Church.

The trouble was a threatened split in the Church on the policy to be adopted towards Gentile converts. For the Jewish party, the Gospel was primarily a Jewish concern. They insisted that Gentile converts must enter the Church by the Jewish door—by the acceptance of circumcision and the obligations of the Law. To the advanced wing in Antioch represented by Paul and Barnabas, this view was impossible. It stultified Paul's whole conception of Christianity, and if it had won the day, would have ended Paul's dream of 'the Empire for Christ'.

Thus, in the year 49 or 50, the first great Church Council was convened in Jerusalem to deal with this issue (Acts 15). The result was a compromise embodied in a decree that Gentile converts should abstain from (1) food offered to idols; (2) the taste of blood; (3) the flesh of strangled animals and (4) sexual vice. Though the decree was probably a disappointment to him, Paul evidently interpreted it as giving him all the freedom he needed for his work.

The Second Journey (Acts 15.36–18.22)

Paul was not long back in Antioch when he was proposing a second journey to Barnabas. But when

Barnabas suggested that Mark 'the deserter' should accompany them, Paul demurred and the two friends quarrelled. Barnabas went off to Cyprus with Mark, and Paul choosing Silas (Silvanus) began his second journey, the most momentous of all because in the course of it he took the Gospel to Europe.

Setting off overland through Cilicia they revisited the cities of South Galatia where they left copies of the decree and enlisted Timothy. The trio travelled west-north-west, avoiding Asia and Bithynia, to Troas on the coast near the site of 'windy Troy'. There Paul had a dream. In it a man from Macedonia seemed to implore him, 'Come over and help us.' So Paul and his friends took ship for Macedonia—and Europe. (Was the man from Macedonia Luke, as Ramsay suggests? At this point in the narrative, at any rate (Acts 16.10), we find the first 'we passage'. Here, we infer, Luke the author of the travel-diary, joined the company.)

They began their mission in Philippi, a Roman colony, where Paul's cure of a clairvoyant slave-girl led to their imprisonment. Released by an earthquake they pushed westwards to Thessalonica (modern Salonika) where they must have spent some time. One again their preaching roused Jewish rancour, and they had to go on to Beroea, where the same thing happened. So leaving his two friends to settle affairs in the young churches, Paul went south to Athens. Here alone he had little success. The *flâneurs* of Athens were in no mood to give a serious hearing to the little Jew with his strange gods, and his philosophical speech to the court of the Areopagus missed fire.

And now Paul struck west to the great commercial city of Corinth. Here he fell in with Aquila (a tent-maker like himself) and his wife Priscilla (clearly a notable woman)[1] who had recently been expelled along with other Jews from Rome by the Emperor Claudius. Eighteen months he stayed in Corinth; in spite of Jewish opposition his work prospered; and he was re-joined by Silas and Timothy with news of the Church in Thessalonica which moved him to write the two *Epistles to the Thessalonians* on the Second Coming of Christ. When the new Roman governor, Gallio, arrived in A.D. 51 (a date which we know from the Delphi inscription) the Jews tried to accuse Paul before the authorities; and though the governor, with an Olympian indifference that has become proverbial, sent the Jews about their business, Paul left Corinth and after making a brief halt *en route* at Ephesus, returned to his headquarters at Antioch.

The Third Journey (*Acts 19–21.17*)

Before long Paul was on the road again. He had promised to revisit Ephesus, and thither he now went, via Asia Minor, after revisiting his churches in Galatia. Here he spent three years. It was during the time that disturbing news from Corinth made him write *The First Epistle to the Corinthians*. In Ephesus his labours bore rich fruit; the Gospel spread to the country all round Ephesus, and even to Colossae and Laodicea in the Lycus valley. But again trouble arose—this time from the makers of Artemis-images (the city with its temple being the centre of the cult of Artemis) whose revenues had not been improved by Paul's preaching against idolatry. Paul's life was in danger: so much is clear; but

[1] This Christian couple are mentioned six times in the New Testament, and in four of these passages Priscilla's name stands first.

it is also possible that he suffered an imprisonment here of which Acts says nothing, and just possible that one or more of the Prison Epistles came from Ephesus, and not, as tradition says, from Rome.[1]

Paul left the city, went north, and crossed to Macedonia and Greece on a tour of inspection. While in Macedonia he wrote *The Second Epistle to the Corinthians*, having heard that the trouble in Corinth was taking a turn for the better. Then he went on in person to Corinth and stayed there for three months. It was during this time that, his thoughts turning westwards, he wrote *The Epistle to the Romans* in order to pave the way for his projected visit.

Meanwhile, however, a debt of honour remained to be paid. For some time he had been making a collection among his Gentile churches for the poverty-stricken mother-Church; and he now resolved to accompany the delegates of these churches to Jerusalem, hoping hard that this gesture of goodwill might mollify his enemies there. Returning, therefore, via Philippi and Troas, he had a poignant meeting with the Ephesian elders at Miletus (see Acts 20) before resuming his journey by sea to Jerusalem.

The Last Journey: Jerusalem, Malta, Rome

Though warned of the risk, Paul went up to Jerusalem. When James, the Lord's brother, and now head of the mother-Church, advised him to conciliate the Jews by joining in a Temple vow, he obeyed; but 'some Jews from Asia', alleging that he had desecrated the Temple, attacked and would have killed him but for the intervention of the commander of the Roman garrison. A

[1] See G. S. Duncan, *St. Paul's Ephesian Ministry.*

speech by Paul failed to pacify the angry mob; and when Paul appeared before the Sanhedrin, the only result was a quarrel between Pharisees and Sadducees, and Paul found himself again in the Roman barracks. At last, the commander hearing, through Paul's nephew of a plot against his life, packed Paul off under escort to the Roman governor at Caesarea. His accusers followed him there, but when they failed to convince Felix, the governor deferred judgment indefinitely, and kept his prisoner in prison for two years until Festus, his successor, arrived.

The arrival of Festus encouraged Paul's enemies to make a further attempt to get his case transferred to Jerusalem for trial. Paul, realizing that this could only mean death for him, played his last card: 'I appeal unto Caesar.' That word uttered, Paul passed out of Festus' jurisdiction: all that Festus could now do was to send him to Rome.

'I must also see Rome,' Paul had once said. His wish was now fulfilled, though in circumstances far other than he had expected. *En route* for Rome, his ship ran into a heavy storm off Crete (see Acts 27, one of the most vivid storm-pieces in literature), and after being tempest-driven in the Adriatic, was wrecked on Melita (Malta). Three months they wintered there, and then proceeded by stages to Rome. But Caesar was in no hurry to judge Paul, and for two years he was kept in open confinement in Rome. It was during this time that he wrote the Prison Epistles: *Colossians, Ephesians, Philemon,* and *Philippians.*[1]

Here the narrative of Acts comes to a close. Paul's end is uncertain. One tradition declares that when he

[1] See note on *Paul's Ephesian Ministry,* p. 89

was tried, he was acquitted, and, on release, resumed his travels, only to be rearrested. (To this period would belong the *Pastoral Epistles*, if we could believe them genuine.) It is likelier, however, that at the end of the two years mentioned in Acts either the Neronian persecution broke out, or there came that change in Roman policy towards the Church which produced the persecution, and that Paul fell a victim to the ensuing 'purge'. Tradition has it that he died at a place called Three Fountains on the Ostian Way. There one swift sword-stroke, and the Apostle of the Gentiles left for ever the body of humiliation, and stood before his Lord delivered from the body of corruption into the glorious liberty of the children of God, in a body made like unto the body of Christ's glory, but which would for ever bear upon it the marks of the Lord Jesus.

Note on Paul's Ephesian Ministry

We have assumed, with the early Church, that Paul's four Prison Epistles, including Philippians, came from Rome. But is it possible that Paul wrote them from an Ephesian prison?

Let us briefly state the case for Ephesus and against Rome. The first thing is to weaken the link with Rome by asking the question: Is it likely that the ten friends of Paul named at the end of Colossians and Philemon *all* followed him to Rome? The next point is the consideration that Ephesus, only 100 miles from Colossae, was a likelier place of refuge for the runaway Onesimus than Rome 800 miles distant. True, but Acts says nothing about Paul being imprisoned in Ephesus. Yet Luke's narrative in Acts is far from exhaustive, and odd bits of evidence in Paul's letters suggest that 'the half has not been told'. Consider passages like I Cor. 15.32 ('I fought with beasts at Ephesus') and II Cor. 1.8 ('the affliction we experienced in Asia'), and add to them the Marcionite Prologue to Colossians: 'Paul, now in bonds, is writing to them from Ephesus'.

Suppose, then, a *prima facie* case for Ephesus has been made out. Do the contents of the Prison Epistles themselves favour it?

What about Colossians and Philemon? Luke was with Paul when these two letters were written. We know that Luke was with Paul in Rome, but we do not know that Luke was with Paul in Ephesus. The case for linking these two letters with

Ephesus is thereby weakened. But is there anything in Philippians for supposing it came from Ephesus rather than Rome?

(1) We must no longer say that the references to 'the Praetorium' (Phil. 1.13) and to 'the saints of Caesar's household' (4.22) necessarily mean Rome. 'Praetorium' often means 'Government House' and 'Caesar's household' was a kind of Imperial Civil Service. Ephesus had both of these.

(2) The frequent comings and goings between Paul's prison and Philippi (see Phil. 2.25 ff.) may be said to suit Ephesus better than Rome. (Rome to Philippi took about 60 days; Ephesus to Philippi about 10.)

(3) The travel-plan coincidence of Phil. 2.19 and Acts 19.22 appears to tell in favour of Ephesus. In the first passage Paul plans to send Timothy to Philippi in Macedonia; in the second, Paul sends Timothy to Macedonia.

These are undoubtedly good arguments for linking Philippians with Ephesus—if only we could be sure that Paul was imprisoned there. If we could, we might date Philippians about 55 instead of in 62.

XII

The Gospel According to St Paul

THE earliest Gospel, Mark, was written in Rome just after the Roman Government had begun to persecute the Christian Church there on the rather flimsy excuse that they had set the city on fire. The date of its writing was probably a little after 65. About nine or ten years before this, a visitor to Corinth might have found a little Jew busily dictating a letter to those Christians in Rome. He was taking great pains over this particular composition; and when he had finished it, he found that he had used up about twelve feet of a papyrus roll.

The little Jew's name was, of course, Paul, and his long letter has, by good fortune, come down to us. It is the Epistle to the Romans, and of all Paul's letters perhaps best merits the name of 'epistle'. If a sub-title were to be found for it, we could not do better than 'The Gospel according to St Paul', because in his letter Paul deliberately set himself to expound the Gospel as he understood it. (Not that Paul's Gospel was radically different from the Gospel which the other apostles preached—the very suggestion he would have hotly repudiated—but rather it was the one apostolic Gospel passed through the alembic of his own original mind, and signed and countersigned by his own experience.)

The Writer and his Readers

Nobody knows who founded the Church in Rome. We guess that it arose through the infiltration of Christian travellers into the capital, and infer from Romans

that though it contained Jews, its members were mostly
Gentiles (see, e.g., 1.5-7, 13-15). A large Church it must
have been when Paul wrote to it, for less than a decade
later the Christians in Rome could be described as 'an
immense multitude' (Tacitus), and represented as a public danger. But if Paul had not founded this Church, he
had friends in it, and he had long cherished the dream
of visiting Rome (1.13). As he sojourned in Corinth (on
the third journey), it looked as if at last his dream were
coming true. He was just about to start for Jerusalem
with a collection for the poverty-stricken Christians
there; but, that visit paid, he planned to 'go west', to
Rome and even Spain (15.24). So, summoning his
amanuensis Tertius (16.22), he dictated a letter to 'all
that are in Rome, beloved of God, called to be saints',
his purpose being to pave the way for his projected visit,
and perhaps to enlist their help for his Spanish mission
(15.24).

The Letter Itself

Romans is in places 'heavy going'. (Was the author of
Second Peter thinking of it when he complained that in
the epistles of 'our beloved brother Paul' there are 'some
things hard to be understood'?) The truth is that Paul
was handling mighty themes—thinking out God and the
world and life and death—in the light of the new fact
of Christ—and it was not always easy to express his
thoughts in simple and intelligible terms. Besides, many
of his thought-forms and metaphors (for example, those
from the slave-market and the law-court) do not come
so cogently home to us as they must have done to his
first readers. These difficulties can be overcome by reading Romans in Moffatt's translation (nowhere is Moffatt
happier than in his renderings of the Pauline epistles)

and by using a good modern commentary like that by C. H. Dodd. All that we can attempt here is to give some idea of the general march of Paul's argument.

What is Romans all about? The answer can be put in six words: 'Salvation, its root and its fruit' (Anderson Scott). We can divide the Epistle up into five parts:

The Prologue (1.1-15).
Salvation, its root (1.15–8.39).
Philosophy of History (chs. 9–11).
Salvation, its fruit (ch. 12–15.13).
The Epilogue (15.14–16.27).[1]

Omitting the Prologue and the Epilogue, to which we have already alluded, let us consider the three main sections of the letter.

1. Paul begins by stating the central truth of the letter (1.16), that in the Gospel, which he defines as 'a saving power', a way of getting right with God has been provided by God Himself, and is open to faith and faith only. But do all men need this 'rightness with God'? Yes, says Paul, for all, Jews and Gentiles alike, have sinned by breaking God's law. But surely the Gentiles never had a law of God? Yes, they had an eternal principle of right and wrong written in their consciences. Nor is the Jew in any better case. He has had God's Law—His revelation of His holy will—in the Mosaic Law, and he has not kept it. Thus all men alike are guilty at the Divine Bar and stand in need of 'justification' or 'acquittal' (Paul's forensic term for 'forgiveness')

---

[1] Some scholars believe that chapter 16, which is a succession of 'salutes', was not originally a part of Romans, but a separate letter to commend Phoebe, a deaconess from Cenchreae, to the Church in Ephesus. Moreover, there is some manuscript evidence to suggest that Romans circulated, either in Paul's time or after it, minus chapters 15 and 16. For a discussion of these technical points the reader should consult the commentaries.

But how is a man to get right with God? By trying
to keep a lot of rules and regulations? By trying to
lay up a satisfactory credit balance of works in the
ledgers of heaven? No; these things, however hard he
try, man cannot do. Is then man's case completely hope-
less? God forbid; for it is just here that the Gospel
comes in. Its message is that God of His free grace has
provided the means of forgiveness through the redemption wrought in Christ. When man by faith accepts this
forgiveness God gives him the power to lead a new life
in a society of redeemed people called the Church. Faith
is the utter trust of man in this gracious God, and
Abraham is the classic example of the man who thus
took God at His word and was 'justified'. Thus forgiven,
we have peace with God and enjoy the hope of glory,
with no fear of the wrath to come. But that does not
mean that we, having been thus forgiven, may persist in
sin. At baptism we turned our backs on sin, and in
Christ died to sin and rose to newness of life. Henceforward we must try to live out what we really are—the
redeemed and forgiven children of God. (Chapter 7
vividly describes the terrible Jekyll-and-Hyde struggle
that goes on in man until he finds salvation in Christ.)
This life is one of sonship to God by adoption, the con-
trolling power of which is the Holy Spirit; and though
suffering may be our present lot, it is as nothing com-
pared with the glory to be revealed; for nothing in this
world, or out of it, can separate us from the love of God
made manifest in Jesus Christ our Lord (1.16–ch. 8).

2. In chapters 9–11 Paul turns to discuss a burning
question, Why have the Jews, God's chosen People, rejected Christ? and in so doing gives us his *philosophy
of history*. His answer to the question is twofold: first,
God is absolute sovereign and can do with His own as

He wills—can for His own ends will that His ancient
People should meantime reject the Gospel. In the
second place, he emphasizes the fact of human responsibility: if the Jews have rejected the Gospel, they have
done so deliberately—by their own faithlessness. But he
cannot end on this note of despair, and his final chapter
(11) declares that the rejection of the Jews is all part of
God's great plan; and when the Gentiles have been
saved, God will save the Jews too. He concludes with
a hymn in praise of God's wisdom: 'O the depth of the
riches both of the wisdom and knowledge of God! How
unsearchable are his judgments and his ways past finding out! For of him, and through him, and unto him
are all things. To him be glory for ever and ever. Amen.'

3. Paul always ends his letters on a practical note.
Having begun with the root of salvation he now ends
with its fruit. In other words, having expounded the
doctrine of the matter he goes on to show how it ought
to work out in daily living. Truth for Paul is always
'truth in order to goodness'. So, in chapters 12–15.13,
he describes the kind of life and conduct expected of
those who have by faith accepted the Gospel.

All must live together harmoniously as members of
Christ's Body, each man using to the full the gift God
has given him; and love must inspire all their thinking
and doing. They must submit to all legally constituted
civil authority, owing no man anything save the debt of
love; and, because the night is far spent, cast off the
works of darkness and put on the armour of light.
'Weak' brothers (that is, those whose minds are still
vexed with petty scruples about food and other things)
must receive tender consideration from the 'stronger'
brethren who exult in their Christian liberty; and all
must learn to bear each other's burdens. So may the

God of hope fill them with all joy and peace in believing (ch. 12–15.13).

Then, with some account of his future plans and greetings to his friends, Paul ends his letter.

Theologically, this is the most important of all Paul's epistles. Coleridge pronounced it 'the most profound work ever written'. Calvin said that it 'opened the door to all the treasures in the scriptures'. Luther called it 'the chief book of the New Testament and the purest Gospel'. What is there in Romans to justify these exalted verdicts? Surely it is that in Romans we have the answer to the question, 'What is Christianity?' by the strongest thinker in the early Church. Moreover, it is a striking fact that whenever there has been a really great revival in the Christian Church, it has generally been associated with the rediscovery by someone (Augustine, Luther, Barth) of the essential message of Romans. Written nineteen hundred years ago, the Word of God which it contains still has power to move men to repentance and faith. For the case of man is as desperate as ever, and all our man-made panaceas are impotent to cure it. The divine remedy remains—the remedy that Paul expounds so profoundly in Romans; for in the Gospel of 'the righteousness of God' revealed in Jesus Christ is the one convincing proof that God has not left man in his lost estate, but has come to his rescue in Christ Jesus. In that Gospel is the one assurance for sinful man that for his sin there is forgiveness, for his hurt there is healing, for his weakness there is power, and for his troubled heart there is peace.

> 'Long, long ago the Truth was found,
> A company of men it bound.
> Grasp firmly then—that ancient Truth.'

XIII

The Church of God in Vanity Fair

NOWADAYS any schoolboy interested in etymologies associates Corinth with currants. But nineteen hundred years ago it was not comestibles, but culture and courtesans that the word suggested in the popular mind. For 'Corinthian words' implied pretensions to philosophy and letters, and to 'Corinthianize' was polite Greek for 'go to the devil'. The other remarkable thing about Corinth was its cosmopolitan character. In this great commercial city with its half-million inhabitants, situated on the Isthmus of Corinth, dwelt men of all races, bond and free—Greeks, Romans, Jews and 'barbarians'—all sorts of trades prospered, and many cults and religions had their devotees. It has been called 'a compound of Newmarket, Chicago and Paris' with perhaps a bit of Port Said thrown in. To the Christian community in this great heathen city—'the Church of God in Vanity Fair', as someone has picturesquely phrased it—Paul wrote the letter, First Corinthians, which is the subject of this chapter.

Paul's Contacts with Corinth

Modern scholars believe that Paul paid *three* visits to Corinth and wrote *four* letters to it. Here, briefly, is the story as they reconstruct it.

About A.D. 50 Paul founded the Church in Corinth during the second missionary tour (Acts 18.1 ff.); and after he had gone Apollos, the eloquent Alexandrian,

7

continued his work with good success. Later, when Paul was in Ephesus for three years, he heard of some moral laxity in Corinth and wrote what we may call 'the previous letter' to them about it. (See I Cor. 5.9. Part of this letter may be preserved in II Cor. 6.14–7.1, which seems out of place in its present context.) A little later he heard news of further trouble in Corinth, and, about the same time, received a rather complacent letter from Corinth asking his advice on various matters of Christian faith and practice. In reply, he wrote his second letter, our First Corinthians. The trouble did not clear up, and Paul was compelled to pay a second visit—a painful one—to Corinth. Even this did not achieve its end, and when Paul returned to Ephesus he wrote a 'severe' letter to Corinth. (The 'painful' visit, unrecorded in Acts, is inferred from II Cor. 13.1 ff. The 'severe' letter is inferred from II Cor. 2.3 f. and 7.8 ff.; part of it may be preserved in II Cor. 10–13, which is certainly 'severe'.) Later still, after Paul had crossed from Ephesus to Macedonia, he received, through Titus, better news of affairs in the Corinthian Church; whereupon, much cheered, he penned our Second Corinthians —or, perhaps, the first nine chapters. Not long afterwards he paid his final visit to Corinth, during which, incidentally, he wrote *Romans*.

The Letter Itself

A glance at the following table of contents will show the number of perplexing problems Paul had to solve in this letter:

I. *Greetings and Thanksgiving:* 1.1-9.

II. *Paul's judgments on certain abuses reported to* him: 1.10–6.20.

(*a*) Party-strife (1.10–4.21).

(*b*) Immorality (ch. 5 and 6.12-20).

(*c*) Litigiosity (6.1-11).

III. *Paul's answers to questions raised by the Corinthian letter:* chs. 7–15.

(*a*) Marriage problems (ch. 7).

(*b*) The eating of sacrificial food, etc. (chs. 8–10).

(*c*) The veiling of women at public worship (11.1-16).

(*d*) Scandals in the Corinthian Lord's Supper (11.17-34).

(*e*) Spiritual Gifts (chs. 12–14).

(*f*) Difficulties about the resurrection (ch. 15).

IV. *Business, News and Greetings:* ch. 16.

After the greeting and thanksgiving Paul deals at once with the evils which had been reported to him by 'Chloe's people'. Like the preacher in the sermon laconically reported to his wife by Calvin Coolidge, he is emphatically 'against' them.

To begin with, he had heard of distressing party-strife in the Corinthian Church. Factions had arisen: some stood by Paul, their first father in God; others who admired his eloquent divinity, were for Apollos; others again swore by Peter as one of the original apostles (for some doubted 'the validity of Paul's orders'); while there were some who, disdaining all human intermediaries, call themselves 'the Christ party'. Here were 'unhappy divisions' indeed; and Paul had not only to prick the bubble of their spiritual pride, but to recall them to the truth that 'one is your Master, Christ', and that even apostles, though they bore exalted names and were never so eloquent, were but servants of Christ, and stewards of the Gospel.

Then he had learned of a Christian living in open sin with his father's wife. This grave sin the Corinthians had complacently condoned. Paul peremptorily bids them excommunicate the offender: they must clean out the bad leaven, and dissociate themselves from all such people.

Finally, he rebukes their reported litigiosity. Why, he asks, do they dare to take their law-suits before heathen courts? At the very least they ought to settle such quarrels among themselves; but they would do better to suffer such injuries without thought of legal action. He ends his first section with another stern warning against sexual sin: 'Know ye not,' he says, 'that your body is a temple of the Holy Spirit in you which ye have from God?'

In the second main section (7–15) Paul deals mostly with the questions put in the Corinthian letter. The first concerned Christian marriage. To marry, or not to marry, in view of existing conditions? Are separation and divorce permissible to a Christian, especially if one of the partners is a pagan? What about 'spiritual marriages' (the curious custom whereby a man and a woman lived together as brother and sister, and not as husband and wife)? These were some of the questions involved. Paul's general answer may be summed up something like this: 'Ideally, celibacy is best. But marriage is better than the fever of passion. Divorce followed by remarriage is not permissible. A widow may be remarried, but only to a Christian.'

The next question was: Is it right for a Christian to eat meat that has been consecrated to idols? (A burning question, for most of the meat on sale in the butchers' shops must have been of this sort.) And there was the cognate question: May a Christian accept invitations to supper-parties in heathen temples? Apparently the Corinthians had argued: 'We have knowledge: we know that these idols are not real. Therefore we can do what we like in this matter.' To this Paul replies: 'Granted. All things are lawful for a Christian, but all things are not advisable; and the wise course for you "knowledgeable" people is to forgo your Christian rights if they cause offence to your weaker brethren who still have scruples about this food.' He goes on (in chapter 9) to show how he himself had forgone many of his Christian rights that 'he might cause no hindrance to the Gospel'. Let them not imagine that because they have the Christian sacraments they can go anywhere and do anything. The Jews in the wilderness had their sacraments too, but that did not prevent God punishing them for their moral declensions. Participation in pagan supper-parties is dangerous: 'You cannot drink the cup of the Lord and the cup of devils.' 'All things are lawful,' he concludes, 'but all things edify not.'

The next question was: Should women be veiled in Church? After answering 'yes' and adducing arguments from theology and nature, he proceeds to discuss the reported scandals in the Corinthians' Lord's Supper. Apparently at this church-supper which was a common meal (probably in the evening) with the Holy Communion as its central point, the richer members of the church were treating their poorer brethren with contumely: while the latter starved, the rich were guilty of gluttony and even drunkenness; and all this was happening at what should have been a very sacred meal.

'People who behave like that,' Paul replies, 'ought to eat at home. This meal which some of you are turning into an orgy is the *Lord's* Supper. Don't you remember what I told you, on the Lord's authority, about its origins? Unless you have a reverent sense of what you are doing at it, you will be guilty of grave sin against the Host at the Supper. The heavy death-rate among you recently is a sign of the divine displeasure at your sacrilegious conduct.'

Paul then turns to discuss the 'spiritual gifts' of which the Corinthians were very proud. *All* the activities of the community, he argues, are due to the Spirit, and this unity of the Spirit corresponds to the unity of the Body of Christ, which is the Church. Like the members in the body, all gifts—even the less showy ones—have their true place in the Church. But of all the gifts the finest is love. Without it the others are worthless. Other gifts will pass away; it alone will abide, for love is the life of heaven.

As between prophecy (a sort of inspired preaching) and 'speaking with tongues' (wild ecstatic speech under the stress of religious emotion) the former is to be preferred; for it edifies, and the other does not. In the interests of orderly worship—God is a God of peace and not of confusion—they must strictly limit the numbers of those who prophesy and those who speak with tongues. No; women must not be allowed to speak in church. Finally, their guiding rule in these things should be: 'Let all things be done decently and in order.'

The last topic Paul handles is the resurrection. Apparently the Corinthians' worry was not over Christ's resurrection or the general belief in a future life, but

over 'the resurrection *of the body*'. Paul begins by
citing the historical evidence for Christ's resurrection
(our earliest documentary evidence); proceeds to a
reductio ad absurdum: 'If there is no resurrection of
the body,' he says, 'as some of you say, Christ cannot
have been raised; and if he is not risen, you are still in
your sins and the Christian message of salvation a false-
hood. But, as a matter of fact, Christ is risen, and the
risen Christ is the pledge that all who are "in Christ"
shall rise too.' Then he faces the question: 'What sort of
body will the dead have when they are raised?' His
argument, buttressed by analogies from nature, is that
as man has now a natural body—an organism adapted
to the conditions of this life—so hereafter he will get a
spiritual body—an organism adapted to the conditions
of the spiritual world. 'Don't misunderstand me,' he says
in effect, 'I am not teaching a resurrection of relics. At
the Second Advent of Christ, God will give us *new*
spiritual bodies, and this mortal will put on immortality.'

Then with a reference to the collection he was raising
among the Gentile churches for the mother-Church in
Jerusalem, a promise that he will visit them soon, a
commendation of Stephanas, and a handful of greetings,
he concludes: 'My love to you all in Christ Jesus.'

If Romans shows us Paul as theologian, First Corinthians reveals Paul the administrator; and no epistle
better illustrates his own phrase 'that which cometh
upon me daily, the care (worry) of all the churches'.
Preachers sometimes bid us cast our eyes back to the
halcyon days of the early Church; but in Corinth at
least, life was no happy, care-free idyll. What this letter
reveals is the impact of the Christian Faith on the low
moral life of a great pagan city, and the hundred and

one problems that consequently arose for the sincere believer. But we see in the letter also one who has a triumphant belief in the adequacy of the Gospel to solve all problems, and who gives us solution after solution according to the grace vouchsafed to him. Sometimes his arguments do not convince us (thus, e.g., we feel that Paul never understood what a happy Christian marriage could be, and in his attitude to women we may judge him a trifle 'obscurantist'); yet we cannot read First Corinthians without marvelling again and again at the deep Christian wisdom and tact of the apostle; and the principles he lays down (as, for example, 'all things are lawful, but not all things are expedient') are capable of wide application. But, these things apart, the two pre-eminent glories of the letter are the thirteenth chapter with its superb hymn in praise of Christian love, and the great and comfortable words of the fifteenth chapter on the resurrection.

XIV

The Trials and Triumphs of an Apostle

THE letter is II Corinthians, but we might also have entitled it, more tersely, 'Apostolic Autobiography', for no letter of Paul's—not even Galatians—tells us more than this one about Paul himself (as distinct from his views). 'Here broken sharply off, with none of the jagged edges filed down, is a chunk of Paul's life— authentic, uncensored, bewilderingly complicated, but amazingly interesting.'[1] But, as this same writer says, reading II Corinthians is like turning on the radio in the middle of a difficult play. Characters are speaking, things are happening; but we cannot always be sure who the people are, or what precisely is going on. Nevertheless, we are not quite in the dark, for the letter itself lets fall a number of clues, and by a little detective work we can solve most of the major problems.

To begin with, we must recall, and amplify, what was said about Paul's contacts and correspondence with Corinth. I Corinthians was written from Ephesus about A.D. 55. We know from Acts 20.1-3 that Paul later visited Corinth before going up to Jerusalem with the collection he had been taking in his churches for the needy Christians in Judea. But the clues in II Corinthians show that, between the writing of I Corinthians and the Acts 20 visit, Paul not only visited Corinth again but wrote at least one letter to it.

This is evidently what happened. After the receipt in

[1] R. Hanson, *II Corinthians*, p. 7

Corinth of I Corinthians (and because of it?) some sort of rebellion against Paul's leadership broke out in the church there. It was led by some Jewish Christians (11.22 f.) who called themselves 'apostles' and came with letters of recommendation (3.1). The situation grew so bad that Paul was compelled to hurry from Ephesus to Corinth (2.1; 12.14; 13.1 f.). But his visit proved painful (2.1), and he had to return without quelling the revolt. Back in Ephesus he determined to try what writing would do; so a severe letter was sent, ordering the Corinthians to mend their ways and punish the rebels (2.3, 4, 9). Titus carried this letter, and Paul, waiting anxiously for the result, moved from Ephesus to Troas and then over into Macedonia. There (2.13) Titus turned up, and the news he brought from Corinth was splendid. The situation had improved immensely. The Corinthians had punished a local ringleader in the trouble (2.5-11), and rebellion had given place to 'godly grief' (7.9 f.). So Paul sat down and wrote a thankful letter to Corinth. This is our II Corinthians—or possibly II Cor. 1–9.

Why this qualification? We spoke a moment ago of a 'severe letter'. Has anything of it survived? Nobody who reads II Corinthians attentively can fail to note the abrupt change of tone that comes over the letter after the ninth chapter. Up till then Paul's tone has been one of thankfulness and reconciliation. But at 10.1 the thankfulness suddenly changes to a fierce defence of his apostleship and an equally fierce denunciation of some men as 'false apostles' and servants of the devil. If these four fierce chapters at the end of II Corinthians were part of the 'thankful letter', they must have completely spoiled the eirenic purpose of the first nine chapters.

And therefore (though there is no MS evidence for the break) it is commonly held that II Cor. 10–13 are a part of the 'severe letter' which followed the painful visit. Both the 'severe letter' and the 'thankful letter' must have been written fairly close to each other—let us say in the year 56.

II Corinthians may be analysed as follows:

I. *Greeting and Thanksgiving:* 1.1-11.
II. *Paul's Relations with the Corinthians:* 1.12–7.16.
    (a) Defence against the charge of fickleness (1.12–2.17).
    (b) The glory of the apostolic office (3.1–6.10).
    (c) Paul's reconciliation with his converts (6.11–7.16).
III. *The Collection for Jerusalem:* chs. 8–9.
IV. *Paul's Defence of his Character and Work:* 10.1–13.10.
V. *Farewell and Blessing:* 13.11-14.

Paraphrase

Dear People of God in Corinth:

God be praised for comforting us in all our troubles, and especially for his deliverance of me in Asia when I despaired of my life. You think me fickle because I had to change my plans for visiting you? Before God I protest I am not a man to say Yes and No in the same breath. (Our Lord is the Yes to all God's promises.) Not fickleness but the wish to spare you a second painful visit made me change my plans. (Ch. 1.)

My severe letter was really prompted by my love for you. The offender[1] I forgive, and I hope you will do so

---

[1] A Corinthian who had played a prominent part in the revolt.

too—you have punished him enough. How anxious I was when I reached Troas and found no Titus there! So on I went to Macedonia—and now I feel like singing a doxology to God who always leads us in triumph. (Ch. 2.)

I need no testimonials, as some do. You Corinthian converts are mine—a living letter written not with ink but with the Spirit of the living God, not on stone tables but on human hearts. God has made us ministers of a new Dispensation, one of the Spirit, not of the letter, whose glory quite eclipses the old. But, alas, a veil still covers Jewish minds, for it has never dawned on them that the Old Order is done away in Christ. (Ch. 3.)

In this ministry we toil bravely and honestly. It is a ministry of light against darkness—the light of God's glory which once shone in creation and now shines in the face of Christ. Fragile folk the bearers of the Gospel may be, but this only shows that its power is God's, not man's. It is killing work, but God sustains us, even in the most desperate situations; and if in our bodies we manifest Christ's dying, we share the hope of the Resurrection, assured that present brief affliction preludes eternal glory. (Ch. 4.)

A heavenly dwelling is prepared for us; but, whether at home with the Lord, or absent from Him, our aim is to please Him, remembering He is to be our Judge. Christ died in love for us all; in Him God was reconciling the world to Himself; and we are called as His ambassadors to preach His reconciliation to all men. (Ch. 5.)

So accept God's grace now, as you see how we apostles endure all manner of sufferings for your sake. Our heart is open to you. Won't you open yours to us?

(Avoid sinful ties with unbelievers, and keep yourselves from every defilement of body and spirit.[1] (Ch. 6.)) Open your hearts to us! We have wronged nobody, and you know how proud we are of you. How comforted I was when Titus met me in Macedonia, with all his good news about Corinth. Now I have no regrets about my severe letter—it made you repent and revived your zeal, and the joy of Titus confirmed my confidence in you. (Ch. 7.)

About the Collection. Despite their poverty the churches in Macedonia have contributed splendidly. See that you do so too. Remember how our Lord gave up His heavenly riches for your sake, and give all you can. You made the promise a year ago: well, fulfil it now, according to your resources. Titus and the two others who are accompanying him to Corinth have my full backing. (Ch. 8.)

'Achaia has been ready since last year,' I have been telling the Macedonians. So have your gift ready before I come, and let it be generous. God loves a cheerful giver; and by this service you will glorify Him, and the recipients will thank God for you. (Ch. 9.)

Please don't force me when I come to deal sternly with my opponents. I am neither a coward nor a worldling as they say, but a spiritual warrior capturing every thought for Christ. Are they saying, 'He can write powerful letters, but his personal presence is weak'? Then they will find out when I come that my presence can be as formidable as my pen. Are they saying that I am trespassing where I have no right? On the contrary, I keep to the sphere God gave me in Corinth. (Ch. 10.)

[1] Possibly a fragment of 'the previous letter' mentioned in I Cor. 5.9.

Bear with me. My jealous love for you makes me afraid you may be seduced from your devotion to Christ. How easily you let yourselves be hoodwinked by these fine apostles! The fact that I supported myself in Corinth shows up these charlatans in their true colours. You take so much abuse from them that you cannot object to a little bragging by me. Well, then, I am as good a Jew as they—and who among them can boast a record of sufferings for the Gospel like mine? (Ch. 11.)

On this matter of boasting, I could tell you of my rapture, fourteen years ago, into the third heaven; but I prefer to tell you how the Lord used my thorn in the flesh to lead me into a deeper knowledge of His grace. Yet you forced this bragging on me; for if ever a man did the works of an apostle among you, that man was I. Now, ready for my third visit to Corinth, I protest my honesty and my love for you; though I fear I may find the same old sins rife among you. (Ch. 12.)

On this third visit I warn you I will discipline all offenders, and you will find Christ's power as well as His weakness in me His servant. All God's people here greet you, and may Christ's grace, God's love, and the Spirit's fellowship be with you. (Ch. 13.)

Despite its difficulty, this letter has its great moments. One comes in chapters 4 and 5 where Paul describes the griefs and glories of the apostolic ministry. Here we see what suffering may mean to one who finds the key to the world's riddle in Christ, and who knows that God works with him for good even in the bitterest experiences. Paul sees the killing strain of this ministry as the life of the Crucified extended in the suffering of His servant. The result of suffering so borne is as sure as what happened on the first Easter morning. The God who raised Jesus will raise us also. So *nil desperandum!* Our brief affliction preludes an eternal weight of glory, of which the Holy Spirit in our hearts is the 'first instalment'. Christ's love controls us. If any man is 'in Christ', he is a new person. Christ died, the sinless One, by God's appointing, to reconcile a sinful world, and we are His ambassadors calling men to be reconciled to God.

Paul wrote many fine passages, but this surely ranks among his greatest.

XV

Christian Freedom

'THE Epistle to the Galatians,' said Luther, 'is my epistle; I have betrothed myself to it; it is my wife.' It is not hard to understand Luther's affection for this short, passionate, difficult letter. Like Paul, Luther was a liberator; and when you pierce down beneath the historical accidents to the essentials you discover that they were fighting much the same battle—a battle for the very truth of Christianity. The issues in that battle will become clearer as we proceed.

Nobody has ever doubted that Paul wrote this letter —as well might a man doubt that Carlyle wrote *Sartor Resartus*, or Lamb the *Essays of Elia*. But the scholars still do not agree on two points: who the Galatians were, and when the letter was written. We must consider these two questions.

The old view, still maintained by many continental scholars, is that Paul uses the word 'Galatia' in its *geographical* sense. (Here the reader must pause and get a map of Paul's world open before him.) Paul was addressing Christians in places like Ancyra (Ankara) and Pessinus situate in the old northern kingdom of Galatia where Gauls had settled in the third century B.C. If we ask when Paul visited these regions, we are referred to two passages in Acts:

'And they (Paul and Timothy) went through the region of Phrygia and Galatia' (Acts 16.6).

'He went from place to place through the region of

Galatia and Phrygia, strengthening all the disciples'
(Acts 18.23). In confirmation, the 'North Galatianists'
bid us note that, since in Acts, Pisidia, Phrygia and
Lycaonia are geographical terms, Galatia in Paul's letter
must be the same. Moreover, Luke in Acts does not
call Antioch, Lystra and Derbe cities in Galatia—so
why should Paul? Finally, some of them ask us to believe that the fickleness of the Galatians, as evidenced
in Paul's letter, consists very well with their Gallic
origins! As if any nation had a monopoly in this!

The new view, championed by Sir William Ramsay
and practically every scholar in this country, is that
Paul employs the word 'Galatia' in its *political* sense.
'Galatia' signifies the Roman province of that name
(founded 25 B.C.) which embraced, besides the old kingdom, parts of Lycaonia, Pisidia, and Phrygia. In the
south of this province lay the towns of Antioch,
Iconium, Lystra and Derbe which Paul evangelized
during his first missionary journey. It was to the Christians in these places that Paul addressed his letter. This
is the view of the 'South Galatianists' who begin by disputing the North Galatianists' right to appeal to Acts
16.6 and 18.23. These passages (they say) refer to the
parts of Phrygia which had been incorporated in the
Roman province of Galatia; and (they continue) there
is no clear evidence that Paul ever went to the old
kingdom. Indeed, North Galatia, a wild country with
poor communications, was hardly open enough for
Paul's enemies to have dogged his footsteps there. They
go on to point out that Paul assumes in his letter that
Barnabas was well known to the Galatians (as indeed
he was to the towns of South Galatia), and that Gal. 4.14
('you received me as an angel (messenger) of God') may

well refer to the incident at Lystra (Acts 14.12). And they produce one of their strongest arguments when they declare that Paul, the Roman citizen, elsewhere thinks in terms of Roman provinces (Judea, Achaia, etc.) and must be doing the same in his letter to the Galatians.

If 'probability is the guide of life', most of us will agree that it lies with the 'South Galatianists'.

The question of date is harder to settle. On the North Galatian view, the letter was written after the visit of Acts 18.23—i.e. during Paul's third journey (53–56).

On the South Galatian view, it may have been written either before or after the Apostolic Council of Acts 15 (probable date: A.D. 49). Those who put it after usually point to the theological similarities between Galatians and the letters written during Paul's third journey—I and II Corinthians and Romans—as proof that it must have been written at the same time, possibly from Ephesus about 55.

But the really strong argument for putting Galatians before the Council is the letter's complete silence about the Apostolic Decree of Acts 15. This Decree settled the point at issue in Galatia, viz. that Gentile believers need not be circumcised. If Paul had been writing after the Council, all he had to do was to quote it and silence all controversy.

Our view is that Paul was writing before the Council. If this is the truth, Galatians was written 48–49, perhaps at Antioch, perhaps on his way up to Jerusalem for the Council, and thus becomes the earliest of Paul's letters.

The occasion of the letter is not doubtful. Since Paul had left Galatia, certain 'Judaizers' (Jewish Christians zealous to preserve Jewish customs) had appeared there, and were persuading Paul's converts that circumcision and observance of the Law were essential to Christianity. This flatly contradicted Paul's Gospel; so the Judaizers were at pains to vilify Paul's credentials, by saying that he was a trimmer or, at best, a second-hand apostle who had learned everything from Peter and James. Paul wrote at once, and in great passion, to counteract this Judaizing propaganda, to assert his apostolic independence, and to explain the deepest principles of the Gospel.

The Letter

(The first two chapters contain Paul's declaration of his apostolic independence.)

Paul, an apostle by God's appointment, not man's, to the churches of Galatia:

How quickly you have gone back on your call and exchanged the Gospel of grace for another! A curse on all who pervert it! (Are these the accents of a trimmer?) My Gospel, I tell you, had no human origin—it came to me by Divine revelation. I was a perfervid Jew persecuting the Church till God revealed His Son to me. Did I then consult the Jerusalem apostles? No, I went to Arabia, and it was three years before I paid a fortnight's visit to Jerusalem where I met only James and Peter. Then I was gone to Syria and Cilicia. (Ch. 1.)

Fourteen years after, with Barnabas and Titus, I again visited Jerusalem and submitted my Gospel to the authorities. (If Titus was circumcised, I made no sacrifice of principle to the false brethren.) The authorities accepted my Gospel entire; indeed, James, Peter and John gave us their blessing, and agreed that, while they worked in the Home Field, Barnabas and I should go to the Foreign. One request they made, that we should remember the poor, a thing I was keen to do.

Later, at Antioch, I had to rebuke Peter. At first he had fraternized at table with Gentile Christians, but he drew back when James's men appeared from Jerusalem. I said to him, 'If you a Jew live like a Gentile, why do you compel Gentiles to live like Jews? Jews though we are, we know that acceptance with God comes not by doing the Law but by believing in Christ.' Works of Law will never put a man right with God. For myself, I have done with the Law, and my life is one of trust in God's Son who died for me. (Ch. 2.)

(In the next two chapters Paul faces his readers with the doctrinal issue—Christ or the Law?)

You misguided Galatians, tell me, please, what produced your real Christian experience? Was it observance of the Law or faith in Christ? Faith of this kind is as old as Abraham. God accepted him for it, and, as we have a faith like his, we are Abraham's true sons. The Law, which nobody can keep fully, exposes us to God's curse. But Christ's death has delivered us from it, and God's blessing is now open to the Gentiles.

A human covenant, once ratified, cannot be set aside. No more can God's with its promise. His covenant with Abraham had Christ in view, and cannot be annulled by the Law coming four centuries later. The purpose of the Law, a kind of makeshift, was to expose sins as transgressions; but it was quite unable to give life. Custody under the Law was a stage on the way to the eventual realization of God's promise, which makes us, all alike, in Christ, God's sons and heirs. (Ch. 3.)

Once, we resembled children under strict guardians; now, through God's gift of His Son, we have been adopted into His family. Why then do you want to revert to your old religious bondage, with all this fussing about days and seasons?

Take my line, I beg you. Let me recall how kind you were to me, a sick man, on my first visit. Why have you left me now for these false flatterers? See, I am like a mother in labour till Christ is formed in you.

Why, the very Law you rely on shows you wrong. You remember the story in Genesis of Abraham's two sons? Sarah and her son (Isaac) prefigure the religion of freedom, Hagar and hers, the religion of bondage. You, like Isaac, are children of the promise and destined for freedom. (Ch. 4.)

(In the last two chapters Paul reaches the practical issues.)

'Hold fast, then, the liberty Christ has won for you! If you get yourself circumcised, Christ will be no help to you. Faith working through love is all that matters. You made a splendid start. What upset you? Is it a case of 'the little leaven'? Then the bad man, whoever he is, will pay for it.

Freedom, then, but not licence! Serve one another in love, for love is the whole law. Walk by the Spirit, not by the flesh—you will know them by their fruit. Those who indulge the flesh can never be saved; so let the Spirit bring forth its harvest in you. (Ch. 5.)

Please restore an erring brother gently, and bear each others' burdens. Give yourselves no airs, and test your own work. Let the pupil share his material blessings with his teacher. God judges inexorably; so cultivate the harvest of the Spirit, not that of the flesh. One brings life, the other death. And let us do good to all men, especially the members of God's family.

Mark my big letters! The circumcisers are interested only in externals. Why, they do not even keep the Law themselves. All they want is to glory in your flesh. But all I want to glory in is the Cross of Christ which has changed everything for me. The making of new men, not of marks in the flesh, is what matters. Peace be on all who take this way, especially God's People.

As for my troublers, let them note the signs of Christ's ownership on my body, I defy them all.

Christ's grace be with you. (Ch. 6.)

The problem handled in this letter is this: What makes a man a Christian? Is it circumcision and Law-keeping, or faith in Christ? Paul's answer is in Gal. 5.6: 'External things like circumcision,' he says, 'do not matter. What matters is faith active in love.'

This is part of the bigger question, How is a man to get right with God? Is it by keeping the Law—in modern terms, by keeping the Ten Commandments, and living as Christ tells us in the Sermon on the Mount, etc., etc.? No; these things we ought to do, but we cannot. No man can, by his own exertions, put himself right with God. Let mortal man present himself before the holy God clad in all his good works, and the verdict must always be 'Unrighteous'! The way to acceptance with God is not by works but by faith in Christ who has died for our sins. And real goodness is the *result*, and not the prerequisite, of our faith. The Christian life is not some punctilious observance of a mass of rules and regulations, but the living of the Christ-like life by the power of the Spirit.

The precise issues of Galatians—circumcision and the rest—may no longer be live issues with us; but the message of Galatians is still relevant. Whenever any religious rite is made co-ordinate with faith in Christ as the condition of salvation, this epistle becomes a sword of the spirit to strike down the error. Salvation is by faith in Christ alone. Small wonder Galatians has been called 'the Epistle of Christian Freedom' and 'the *Magna Charta* of evangelical Christianity'.

XVI

The Glory of the Church

WERE a contest held to decide the greatest of Paul's letters, many would choose Romans, but some would prefer Ephesians. John Calvin called it his favourite epistle; Coleridge pronounced it 'one of the divinest compositions of man'; Dr John Mackay has said, 'To this book I owe my life', and Dr C. H. Dodd has named it 'the crown of Paulinism'.

It comes therefore as a shock to some when they learn that many scholars refuse the letter to the one man in the early Church apparently capable of writing it and attribute it to a disciple—a 'Paulinist', as the phrase goes. (The most ingenious modern theory[1] is that its author was none other than Onesimus who first gathered Paul's letters together and then wrote Ephesians to serve as an introduction to them.) Why has Paul's authorship come under suspicion?

First, because of its style and vocabulary. Ephesians contains some 90 words not found elsewhere in Paul's letters. When it is retorted that the shorter Colossians (generally admitted to be Paul's) contains 56 such words, the doubters bid us notice that the writer of Ephesians uses words like 'body', 'fullness' and 'mystery', which occur also in Colossians, in a different sense. When this is challenged, they point us to the general style of Ephesians which, with its long, in-

[1] Professor E. J. Goodspeed's.

volved sentences, contrasts strangely (they say) with the terseness and vigour of Paul's normal manner.

But, such stylistic tests being admittedly very fallible, the doubters turn next to the doctrine. Look (they say) at the doctrine of the Universal Church in Ephesians. Where else in Paul's letters will you find its like? Here the usual reply is that Paul undoubtedly held and taught the doctrine of the Church's universal mission, and that what we have in Ephesians is simply the logical and natural development of his thought.

Finally, the doubters invoke the literary links between Colossians and Ephesians. More than one-third of the words and phrases in Colossians reappear in Ephesians, and this and that passage in Ephesians seems patterned on a corresponding one in Colossians. Here we are invited to see the copying hand of a disciple of Paul. But the so-called copying is done with such freedom and subtlety that other people draw the quite opposite conclusion—in Paul's favour. Besides (they add) if Ephesians was written soon after Colossians, would not many of its phrases still be running in Paul's head?

At this point we may state the case for the defence. To begin with, we may ask the doubters what is the point of the passage about Tychicus (6.21 f.) if the letter is not Paul's? This reference has all the marks of genuineness. Next, let us remember the complete unanimity of the early Church about Paul's authorship. The doubt is quite modern: for eighteen hundred years the Church never questioned it. And, finally, if the letter is not Paul's, we must posit the existence in the early Church of a 'Great Unknown' who was Paul's spiritual peer.

Clearly the burden of proof lies with those who deny

Paul's authorship, and unless and until such demonstration is forthcoming, we may wisely follow tradition and ascribe the letter to Paul.

But was Ephesians really addressed to the Christians in Ephesus? The question is posed by two features in the letter itself. First, the omission of the words 'in Ephesus' (1.1) by our oldest and best MSS; and, second, the fact that the writer does not seem to know his readers personally, as Paul undoubtedly knew the Christians in Ephesus. What then? The solution is to regard Ephesians as a circular letter, or encyclical, sent to the Gentile churches in Asia. This would explain not only the lack of the words 'in Ephesus' but the absence of personal greetings at the end. In the original letter Paul would leave a blank space in the salutation, and it would be the duty of Tychicus (who carried the letter) to fill in the appropriate place name, as he went round the various churches.

Few of Paul's letters are easier to analyse than this one. It falls into two main sections, one theological and the other ethical, or practical, thus:

Salutation: 1.1-2.
Doctrinal Section: 1.3–3.21.
 (Here the theme is God's eternal purpose for man manifested in Christ and the Church.)
Practical Section: 4.1–6.20.
 (Here we are told what church membership means for daily living.)
Conclusion: 6.21-24.

We shall now paraphrase it.

Paul to the Christians (in Asia Minor):
God be praised who has given us such transcendent

blessings in Christ! Before creation He chose us, destining us in Christ to become His sons and receive His grace. In Christ we have redemption, pardon and insight into God's purpose to unite all created things in Christ. In this consummation we, who first hoped in Christ, are promised a share, and you who trusted in Him have received the seal of the Spirit as pledge of full and final salvation.

So I thank God for your faith while I pray that He may give you a vision of the splendour of your inheritance, and of the power which raised Christ and set Him in heaven's highest place. This regnant Christ is Head of the Church, which forms His Body, the nucleus of the great unity yet to be. (Ch. 1.)

Once you were dead in sin. Indeed, we were all in like case, since our evil desires and thoughts merited retribution. But God in His love raised us from death to a heavenly life with Christ. By His grace you have been saved, through faith. Not that this faith is your own achievement; it is God's gift.

Once you Gentiles were excluded from the Divine Society and all God's promises. But now Christ by His sacrifice has brought you in. The barrier dividing us was the Jewish Law. But Christ destroyed it, making peace between the hostile sections of mankind so that they now form a new humanity. Outsiders no longer, you belong to God's household. It is like a great building, with apostles and prophets as its foundation and the key-stone Christ. In Him the whole structure is growing into a Temple of God, of which you are a part. (Ch. 2.)

You may have heard how God graciously revealed to me His Secret. Unknown to past generations but now disclosed to the apostles and prophets, it is this: that Gentiles may share, with God's People, in the same Body and the same promises, in Christ. Of this Gospel God made me a minister, though quite unworthy, so that I might preach Christ's riches to the Gentiles. Thus, through the Church, the heavenly powers may learn the manifold wisdom of God. This eternal purpose is now realized in Christ. Do not then despair, be proud rather, that I am in prison.

So I pray the Divine Father that His Spirit may strengthen you inwardly and Christ dwell in your hearts through faith. Thus you may grasp, with all Christians, how wide, deep, long and high is Christ's love for us and may be filled with the divine life. To God be glory in the Church for ever. (Ch. 3.)

Live a life worthy of your calling, humble, patient, loving, and keep the unity of the Spirit which creates the one Body. God is one, the source of all; Christ is one, the Church's Lord; and we share one faith and hope symbolized in the one baptism. The gifts we each have come from the ascended Christ—for the purpose of the Ascension was that the whole universe might know His presence. These varied gifts of ministry making men apostles, prophets, evangelists, pastors, teachers, serve to make better Christians and build up Christ's Body, till it reaches mature manhood and fully expresses what Christ is. So we must not, like children, be misled by crafty teachers; rather, holding the truth in love, we must grow up into Christ, the Body's Head.

No more living like pagans, then. Purblind and godless, they grow callous and plunge into immorality. How different was the way of Christ you learned! So off with the old evil habits, and on with the new life of holiness after God's pattern. Speak truth, not lies. Don't let anger tempt you to sin. Let the thief turn honest man and help the needy. Avoid foul speech which vexes the Holy Spirit. Cease all bitter and malicious talk, and forgive as God in Christ forgave you. (Ch. 4.)

Love with a love like Christ's—to the point of sacrifice. But among God's People never even mention impurity, for no immoral person will get into God's Kingdom. Let nobody fool you. Darkness and light have nothing in common: so live like the children of light you are. Shun the dark deeds of paganism and show them up.

As the hymn[1] says:

> 'Wake up, O sleeper!
> And arise from the dead!
> And Christ will shine upon you.'

Be wise, and make the most of these evil days. Let your stimulus come from the Spirit, not from wine; and as you sing together God's praise, give him thanks for everything in Christ's name.

Mutual subordination is the rule in the Church. As Christ is the Church's Head, so man is woman's. Let wives be subject to their husbands who should love them as Christ loved the Church. (He died so that the Church might be cleansed and perfected.) As a man cares for his own body, so should a husband for his wife. This marriage relation, I may say, is a symbol of the marriage between Christ and the Church, his bride. (Ch. 5.)

Children must obey their parents, and fathers give

[1] A fragment of an early Christian Baptismal hymn.

their children a Christian training. Slaves should obey their masters as they would Christ, and work as men responsible to him as Judge. Let masters treat their slaves correspondingly, knowing that they have a common Master in heaven.

Finally, gird yourselves for the battle against the powers of evil. Put on God's armour—truth as your belt, righteousness as your breastplate, faith as shield. ... Persevere in prayer, and especially for me that I may boldly preach the Gospel whose ambassador in chains I am. Tychicus, whom I am sending, will tell you all about me. Divine blessings be with you. (Ch. 6.)

'The theme of Ephesians,' says C. H. Dodd,[1] 'is the glory of the Church as the society which embodies in history the eternal purpose of God revealed in Christ.' Let us elucidate this in modern terms.

The Eternal Purpose

For Paul a Divine Intention runs through history. The ultimate Reality is a Father, He has a purpose of love for all, and He wills Community. But the cosmos reveals a 'great rift'—demonic powers marring the Divine Order, and sinful men at enmity with one another. Of himself, man cannot repair the rift; only God can, and God purposes to subdue all opposing powers—human and superhuman—to His will, and to create a great unity.

The Centrality of Christ

The Gospel is the Good News of God's unveiled Secret. (This is what Paul means by 'the mystery'. The

[1] *The Abingdon Bible Commentary*, p. 1222.

word signifies a secret Plan in the Divine Mind which is now being disclosed to the world.) This unveiled Secret is Christ, who is not merely the Messiah of the Jews but the Clue to History and the Meaning of the Universe. God's purpose is embodied in Christ's person and in the victory which He wrought by His dying, rising and ascending, and that purpose is the reconciliation of all created things.

The Glory of the Church

The Purpose of God is to be realized through the Church. The Church is the Body of Christ, the social instrument which is to execute God's purpose in the world. The eternal God wills Fellowship; in that Fellowship Jews and Gentiles are now included; and this process will go on till all are reconciled to God in 'the Christ that is to be'.

Such is the theology of Ephesians, but it carries with it also clear moral demands. On those who are members of the Church are laid the Divine Imperatives of 'living in the light', 'imitating God', 'learning Christ', and 'walking in the Spirit'. For Christians are called to put on the Divine armour and to carry the battle with evil to the furthest frontiers of thought and action.

Seen thus, the ecumenical importance of Ephesians is clear, and we do not wonder that it has been called 'the most contemporary book of the New Testament'.

XVII

A Paean from Prison

SOME years ago, just after Martin Niemöller had been thrown into a concentration camp because he chose to obey God rather than Hitler, I was privileged to hear extracts from a letter which he wrote to a friend in this country. One sentence in that letter stuck in my memory: 'In the old days I used to be a bearer of the Gospel,' wrote Niemöller, 'now that Gospel is bearing me.' That sentence and the serenity of the whole letter are all I remember. But when I heard it read, it reminded me of nothing so much as St Paul's Epistle to the Philippians.

This was not surprising; for the circumstances which led to the writing of both letters were very similar. The place of writing was in each case a state prison, as the writers were both of them ambassadors of Christ, in chains for their loyalty to their Lord.

It is the earlier letter, written about A.D. 60, that forms the subject of this chapter. In some ways Philippians is the most beautiful of all Paul's letters. It is also one of the simplest, and anyone who wishes to make a study of these letters could not do better than begin with this one.

How the Letter came to be written

A glance at the map will show that Philippi is a town of Macedonia in north-east Greece: a very famous town

too. Named after Philip of Macedon, the father of
Alexander the Great, it had been the scene of one of the
decisive battles of history. My map has crossed swords
on it at the spot and the words: 'Death-bed of the
Roman Republic.' There, in 42 B.C., the Republicans,
Brutus and Cassius, who had slain Julius Caesar, met
their doom at the hands of the man who was destined
to be on the throne of the Roman Empire when Christ
was born, the Emperor Augustus. But

> 'The tumult and the shouting dies
> The captains and the kings depart;'

and no fanfare of trumpets heralded the arrival there
some ninety years later of a little man, known today to
thousands who have never heard of Philip or Augustus.
That little man was the Apostle Paul.

It was in the course of his second missionary journey
that Paul and his coadjutors crossed the Aegean Sea,
and landed in Europe not far from Philippi. The story
of how he began work in Philippi is told in Acts 16.
The narrative, which is one of Luke's best, culminates
in the imprisonment of Paul and Silas in the local gaol,
their providential release after the earthquake, and the
conversion of their gaoler. Thus Paul sowed the seed of
the Evangel in Philippi, and a fine harvest it was to
yield. In a few years there had sprung up a church there
of which Paul was prouder than of any other.

So the years went past; once and again Paul visited
Philippi (Acts 20.1, 6); and the cause of the Gospel
prospered. At length there came an abrupt ending to
Paul's journeying. He was arrested in Jerusalem and,
after two years' detention, sent to Rome to stand his
trial before the Emperor. Even in that ancient world

9

without radio, telegraph, or a decent postal service, news travelled fast, and one day the Christians in Philippi heard with dismay of Paul's plight. Without more ado they 'put the hat round for him', as we would say, and some weeks later there arrived in Rome a Christian from Philippi called Epaphroditus with news from his old friends—and a present. We may guess how deeply touched the old man was. Unfortunately, Epaphroditus fell ill and had to stay on in Rome. When he recovered, Paul wrote a letter of thanks to the Philippian Christians for the messenger to take back home. That note is the Epistle to the Philippians.

The Letter

Let us paraphrase its contents:

My dear fellow-Christians in Philippi, with all the office-bearers there, Timothy and I send you our greetings. May grace and peace be with you from God our Father, and the Lord Jesus Christ.

I never say my prayers without thanking God for you and your fellowship in the Gospel. God knows how I am longing for you all and praying that you may grow in love and wisdom.

You kindly ask for news of myself. Strangely enough, my imprisonment has meant the advancement of the Gospel and more preaching of Christ. True, not all are doing it from the purest motives, but the main thing is that it is being done. I believe that I shall be released. But what matters is that Christ shall be magnified in me—whether in life or in death. Frankly, I don't know which to prefer. To die and go to be with Christ would be better for me; to stay on here below would be better for you. And that, I think, is what will happen, and you will see me again. However, whether I come or not, you must live worthily of the Gospel, standing firmly together for the Faith and undismayed by your foes. You are privileged, like myself, not only to believe in Christ but also to suffer for His sake. (Ch. 1.)

Now a word about these little rifts in your fellowship. By all your best Christian instincts I urge you to fill my cup of joy full, by agreeing among yourselves. Think of others and be truly humble—like Christ Himself who freely gave up the glory of heaven, and chose the path of humiliation, even to death on a cross. Therefore God highly exalted Him and gave the name above all other names.

Work away at your own salvation: God is with you in it all. On Judgment Day I shall be proud of you. Even if I have to sacrifice my life now, I rejoice, and I bid you do likewise.

Now about my plans. Timothy I hope to send to you soon. He is devoted to you and I have no trustier friend. But I am confident that I will come myself ere long. With this letter I am sending back your messenger Epaphroditus. How worried he was when you heard he was ill! But God mercifully spared him. Give him a warm welcome. (Ch. 2.)

Finally, brethren, rejoice. I was about to close but will repeat what I said before. Beware of these Judaizers! A bad lot they are. Outward marks and privileges are what they take pride in. If it came to that, I could brag about Jewish privileges as much as anyone. But when I became a Christian I gladly forfeited them all. To know Christ and His benefits is the supreme blessing. Not that I feel myself already at the goal; but my one aim is to win the prize of God's high calling in Christ.

So imitate me. Christ has many enemies, sensual and earthly fellows whose doom is ruin. But our citizenship is in heaven, and we wait for our Saviour Christ who shall refashion our poor mortal bodies into heavenly ones like His own. (Ch. 3.)

Stand firm, my dear people, in the Lord. Make it up, you two ladies who are at loggerheads. Rejoice in the Lord! I will say it again: rejoice. Be sweetly reasonable to all; don't worry; bring all your needs to God in prayer. His peace shall guard you. Lastly, fill your minds with true and noble thoughts.

I was deeply touched by your remembrance of me. Not that I ever complain of want; for no matter what the circumstances, I have learned the secret of contentment, and in Christ I have strength for anything. Yet thank you for your gift—not the first you have sent me. With it I have enough, and more than enough. My God shall supply all your wants.

Give my love to all the brethren. The brethren here, especially those in Government House, send their greetings.

The grace of our Lord be with you.

PAUL

The Value of the Letter

Philippians is full of good things: great utterances about the Faith, and intimate little touches that reveal the man.

'For me to live is Christ,' he says, 'and to die is gain' (1.21). That is how the world and life and death appear to this Christ-captured man. Or he will invest the lowliest Christian duty like humility with the loftiest of sanctions (2.1-11). Or in a couple of verses (3.20 f.) he will express the Christian hope: 'For our citizenship is in heaven: from whence also we wait for a Saviour Jesus Christ who shall fashion anew the body of our humiliation that it may be conformed to the body of his glory.' Or he will write a golden sentence like this: 'Whatsoever things are true, whatsoever things are honourable, whatsoever things are just, whatsoever things are pure, whatsoever things are lovely, whatsoever things are of good report; if there be any virtue, if there be any praise, think on these things' (4.8).

But the dominant note of the Epistle is joy. As Bengel said: 'The sum of the Epistle is: I rejoice; do you rejoice.' No less than sixteen times do the words 'joy' and 'rejoice' occur in it. It is a paean from prison. If, as von Hügel once declared, the supreme mark of the saint is 'radiance amid the storm and stress of life', no man has a better right to the title than St Paul.

XVIII

The Cosmic Christ

THE choice of a title for Colossians is difficult. We
might call it 'Paul to the Rescue'—for his readers were
in danger of making spiritual shipwreck: or (borrowing
Alice Meynell's title) 'Christ in the Universe', since the
Cosmic Christ of Colossians is Paul's answer to the
heretics who were troubling the church. But these are
riddling words till we have described Colossae and its
heresy.

Colossae, a city of great antiquity, lay in the Lycus
valley near Laodicea and Hierapolis, a hundred miles
east of Ephesus. The church there had probably been
founded by Epaphras, one of Paul's Ephesian converts.
His friend Philemon also lived there, so that, though
Paul had never visited the city (2.1), he was deeply
interested in the Colossian church.

One day, while he lay a prisoner in Rome, Epaphras
arrived reporting the outbreak of heresy in the church
at Colossae. The general nature of the heresy is clear
enough from Paul's letter. It was a theosophy in which
Judaism, Gnosticism (the pagan 'Higher Thought' of the
time) and Christianity were mixed in one strange hotch-
potch. It certainly had Jewish features, for we read
about new moons, festivals, sabbaths and angel worship
(2.16, 18). No less certainly it possessed Gnostic traits,
since Paul talks of a pernicious 'philosophy' (2.8) traf-
ficking in 'elemental spirits of the universe' (2.8, 20),
and the heretics' cult of asceticism (2.20-23) suggests the

Gnostic belief that matter is something evil with which God—or those who worship Him—can have no contact. Hence the heretics seem to have postulated a hierarchy of spirit-mediators, or powers, strung out between God and the world—a system in which we gather that Christ had a high, but not the supreme, place.

The errors which the heretics were propagating were therefore Christological and ethical. On the one hand, they scaled down the person and work of Christ, robbing Him of His uniqueness. On the other, they were forcing on the Christians in Colossae a false asceticism and futile food-taboos. So, in the Christological part of his reply, Paul had to tell the Colossians that Christ was the 'totality' of Godhead and had done all that was needed for man's salvation; and, in the ethical part, that the Christian life means not a despising of God's good gifts but a clean break with the old bad life and a new life with Christ.

We may analyse the letter thus:

Salutation and Thanksgiving: 1.1-13.
The Person of Christ and His Work: 1.15–2.7.
Warning against Heretics: 2.8-23.
The New Life in Christ: 3.1–4.6.
Greetings and Blessings: 4.7-18.

Paul and Timothy to the Christians in Colossae:

I thank God for your Christian faith and love, founded on the heavenly hope of the Gospel which is spreading in all the world. Epaphras has told me of your love, and my prayer is that you may know God's will and live worthily of Him who rescued us from the powers of darkness and set us in the realm of His dear Son. Christ, the image of God, was in being before creation; the visible and invisible worlds owe their origin to Him; and creation was through and for Him. Moreover, as death's first conqueror, He is the Head of the new creation, the Church, which forms His Body. The totality[1] of Godhead chose to dwell in Him, and, by means of the Cross, to reconcile all warring elements in the universe. You, once strangers from God, share in that reconciliation through the death of the incarnate Christ—if you maintain your faith and hope.

So I rejoice to share in the sufferings of Christ for His Church. God has made known to me His Divine Secret, as it affects the Gentiles. It is 'Christ in you the hope of glory', and into it I toil to initiate every man. (Ch. 1.)

My concern is that you and the Laodiceans (though we have never met) should grow in love and in understanding of this Secret—I mean, Christ, who embodies all the treasures of wisdom and knowledge. Though absent, I know your firm spiritual front. So do not be deceived by any religion based on elemental spirits. Christ gives you all you need for salvation. The true circumcision is that which He made possible—the severance with the old lower nature, when you died and rose with Him in baptism. When you were dead in sin, God gave you new life, and freed you from the demands of the Law which He abolished at the Cross. There He disarmed and defeated all the spirit-powers.

So let nobody fault you on food or holy days or inveigle you into asceticism or angel worship. To allow

---

[1] Col. 1.19; 2.9. The Greek word *plerōma* had probably been used by the heretics. Paul re-employs it to declare that the 'sum total' of the Divine character dwelt in the human personality of Jesus. It is a way of expressing what we call 'the Divinity of Christ'.

this would be disloyalty to the Head who alone gives unity and growth to the Body. Since your conversion you have lost all connexion with these powers. Why then pay heed to the futile prohibitions connected with their worship? (Ch. 2.)

As men risen with Christ, lift your thoughts above, where Christ is. Make an end of all carnal passions, anger, malice, slander and lying. Strip off your old bad self, and put on the new self after God's pattern. (In the new humanity old distinctions of race and caste are finished.) Compassion, kindliness, humility and forbearance are your new virtues, with love to bind them into one. Let Christ's peace rule in your hearts, and His Word dwell in you, as you sing God's praise with hymns and do everything in the name of the Lord Jesus.

In Christian homes, wives must defer to their husbands, and husbands love their wives. As the children must obey their parents, the fathers in turn should treat them gently. Slaves are to obey their masters, not as men-pleasers but as servants of the Lord, and masters are to use their slaves considerately, aware that they too have a Master in heaven. (Ch. 3.)

Include me, please, in your prayers so that, though imprisoned, I may succeed in telling the Secret of Christ. Deal prudently with non-Christians, and show grace and tact when talking to them.

Tychicus, whom I am sending along with the trusty Onesimus, one of yourselves, will tell you how I fare. Greetings from Aristarchus, also in prison, Mark (who may be coming to you) and Jesus Justus—my only Jewish fellow-workers, but what a tonic they have been to me! Greetings also from Epaphras, one of yourselves, who works and prays tirelessly for the churches in the Lycus valley, from the dear doctor, Luke, and from Demas. Remember me to the Christians in Laodicea. When you have read my letter, get it read in Laodicea, and read the one I sent to Laodicea. And bid Archippus get on with his Christian work.

I sign this letter myself. Remember I am in prison. Grace be with you. (Ch. 4.)

What has this letter to say to us to-day? This, to begin with: To all who would 'improve' Christianity (as the heretics proposed) by admixing it with spiritualism, sabbatarianism, anthroposophy, or some sort of 'Higher Thought', it utters a warning. Christ alone is the power and wisdom of God and what He has done is enough for salvation. We need no extra mediators, no taboos, no false asceticism. To piece out the Gospel with the rags and tatters of alien cults is not to enrich but to corrupt it.

And this, second: If the titles and place Paul assigns Christ in this letter surprise and stagger us, they do but say what any true Christology must say, that the Fact of Christ is somehow embedded in creation, which is all there with Christ in view, and that in some deep mysterious way it has the promise of Christ in it.

'I say to thee, the acknowledgement of God in Christ,
 Accepted by the reason, solves for thee,
 All questions in the earth or out of it,
 And has so far advanced thee to be wise.'[1]

[1] Browning.

XIX

Saints in Salonica

MANY men who served in the First World War have memories of Salonica, the sea-port in northern Greece. Nineteen hundred years ago, it was a free city, bore the name of Thessalonica (after Alexander the Great's half-sister), and ranked as the capital of Macedonia. Somebody has said that, wherever Paul went, he caused either a riot or a revival. When, with Silas and Timothy, he arrived there about 49 A.D., he caused both. Unbelieving Jews organized the riot against him when his mission produced a rich harvest of converts, some Jewish, more of them devout Gentiles, plus many of the leading ladies of the town. They were therefore compelled to move on to Beroea where the same thing happened. Acts 17 tells the whole story. At this point Paul went south to Athens, whence he sent Timothy north to find out what was happening in Thessalonica (I Thess. 3.1 f.). He himself went on to Corinth where he stayed eighteen months. While he was there, he was rejoined by his two friends, and Timothy brought a most reassuring report. The young church was in good heart and was standing up bravely to persecution, but one or two points had arisen which needed the apostle's attention. Sexual morality was not all it might be; some converts were idling; and some were worried about what might happen to their friends who died before Christ came. So Paul wrote his first letter to Thessalonica.[1]

[1] Acts 18.5 shows that Silas (=Silvanus) and Timothy shared Paul's work in Corinth. II Cor. 1.19 confirms this. So we may be sure that I and II Thessalonians ('Paul, Silvanus and Timothy', I Thess. 1.1; II Thess. 1.1) were written from Corinth.

We can date it with some precision. The famous Delphi inscription enables us to know that Gallio (Acts 18.12) became proconsul of Achaia (whose capital was Corinth) in the summer of 51. By then Paul had been eighteen months in Corinth (Acts 18.11). He must therefore have arrived very early in 50. Since no long time can have separated his visit to Thessalonica from the writing of the letter, we may safely date it in 50 A.D.

1 Thessalonians

Paul begins by giving thanks for the way in which the Thessalonians had welcomed the Gospel and for their continuing witness to it. (Ch. 1.) Then he begins an apologia (probably in answer to some Jewish insinuations): 'You remember,' he writes, 'our campaign among you. We were completely honest with you; we treated you with great tenderness; we earned our own keep. And you, in your turn, accepted our message as the Word of God, though it has brought you persecution from your fellow countrymen. Have no fear. These wicked men who oppose God's work will be punished.' (Ch. 2.)

Then Paul explains his non-return to them. 'We tried to come back,' he says, 'but we were prevented. So while I stayed in Athens, Timothy came north to find out how you were faring in your troubles. And what good news of you he has now come back with! I can hardly express my relief and joy, or wait to see you again. May God direct me to you.' (Ch. 3.)

Then Paul takes up the points in the report. 'Remember what we taught you,' he says, 'keep your bodies pure, and get on with your work quietly. You ask about your loved ones who have died? Don't despair. When Christ comes in His glory, they will be the first to meet Him.' (Ch. 4.)

'Don't let the rumours about the end of the world upset you. Nobody can tell when the Lord will come. The important thing is that as sons of light you should keep vigilant. Respect your leaders; admonish the idle; always rejoice; and never quench the fire of the Spirit. May God bless and keep you. Greet the brethren with a holy kiss. See that this letter is read to them all. And Christ's grace be with you.' (Ch. 5.)

II Thessalonians

Paul's second letter to Thessalonica, which must have been written very soon after the first one, was designed to clear up some misunderstanding apparently caused by Paul's words concerning Christ's Coming in the first letter. If Paul had given the impression that the Coming was imminent, so that certain of his converts had downed tools, then they must know that certain events must first take place, and meantime there must be no idling.

Paul begins by giving thanks for his converts' steadfastness in persecution. They will be rewarded when Christ comes in glory, as their persecutors will be punished. (Ch. 1.)

Then he reaches his first reason for writing—the prevalence of misconceptions about Christ's Advent. 'Let no one deceive you,' he warns, 'the Day of the Lord has not come—as some are saying—nor will come until the Man of Sin[1] is revealed. Meantime he is restrained; but when he makes his last evil challenge, he will be slain by the Lord Jesus. But you, my readers,

---

[1] II Thess. 2.3. The 'Man of Sin' is Antichrist, a kind of Devil's Messiah who, in the evil days before the End, was expected to war on God and His saints. The something, or someone, who presently restrains him (2.6, 7) is probably the Roman Empire.

God has destined for salvation: so stand firm and hold to the traditions.' (Ch. 2.)

Finally, having asked their prayers for himself, he comes to his second reason for writing—the report that some people had stopped working on the excuse that Christ might return at any time. 'Avoid all such people,' he says, 'this is not what I taught you. What I said was "Work—or want." So settle down, please, and get on with your work. Anybody who disobeys should be ostracized. May the God of peace be with you.'

Then, to authenticate it, he signs the letter in his own hand. (Ch. 3.)

These two letters have been called 'the Cinderellas'[1] in Paul's correspondence. They tend to be ignored because they are undistinguished by any great theological passage and because they contain a mixture of plain commonsense advice and some uncongenial apocalyptic. Yet they shed a vivid light on conditions in one of the very earliest Christian congregations; and when we pierce down to their abiding Christian message, they contain some salutary counsel for us. What do they say? Three things of importance: first, that, if we are looking for a carefree, untroubled life, we have not yet understood our Christian calling; second, that, for Christians, death, however it may come, has lost its sting, for those who are in Christ remain in Him for ever; and, last, that in times of crisis our duty is to hold fast to our rule of life, and get on with our own work.

[1] W. Neil, *Thessalonians*, p. xxvii.

XX

Speaking the Truth in Love

FEW relics throw a more vivid light on the past than old letters. 'That autograph letter,' says Carlyle, 'it was once all luminous as a burning beacon; every word of it a live coal, in its time. It was once a piece of the general fire and light of human life, that letter!' Here is such a letter, written in Egypt about A.D. 298, by one Aurelius Sarapammon to his friend.

'I commission you by this writ to journey to the famous city of Alexandria, and search for my slave by name (the name is lost) about 35 years of age, known to you. When you have found him, you shall place him in custody, with authority to shut him up and whip him, and to lay a complaint before the proper authorities against any persons who have harboured him, with a demand for satisfaction.'

So runs this letter about a runaway slave. Now it happens that there is preserved in the New Testament another letter about a runaway slave written about A.D. 60. The letter is the Epistle to Philemon; and a very human little document it appears, when the story that lies behind it is unfolded.

The Story

The scene of the little drama is laid first in Colossae, a town in the wild heart of Asia Minor, and then in Rome; and the three chief actors are Paul, a citizen of Colossae named Philemon, and his slave Onesimus.

When through Paul's work in and around Ephesus
the Gospel had found its way inland to Colossae, among
the first converts to the Faith were a well-to-do citizen
of the town, Philemon, and his wife Apphia. They were
good Christians, and the local church apparently held
its meetings in their house. But some time before they
had had a bit of domestic trouble: one of their slaves
called Onesimus had helped himself to some of his
master's money, and absconded. No doubt there was a
hue and cry for him, but Onesimus had vanished.
Whither he went on the first stage of his wanderings we
do not know; possibly he made west for Ephesus; but
eventually he turned up hundreds of miles away in
Rome, drifting there, no doubt, as a man to-day in
similar case might drift to London. At last, having
like the Prodigal spent all, he found himself in the
capital

'Homeless in the city, poor among the poor,'

when Providence took a strange but blessed hand in his
fortunes. About this time it chanced that Paul had come
to Rome to stand his trial before the Emperor. One day
the door of his prison opened to admit—Onesimus. We
can imagine Onesimus blurting out with tears the tale
of his sin and shame, and Paul, after a few words of
kindly reproof, telling Onesimus a tale—a tale that he
had told to so many men in so many lands. The sequel
was that Onesimus became a Christian and proved
himself a great source of help and comfort to the
apostle in his bonds.

Paul, however, had come to know Onesimus' past,
and though he loved him dearly, decided that it was his
duty, when opportunity offered, to send him back to his

rightful master. One day not long afterwards the opportunity arrived. A messenger came to Paul's prison all
the way from Colossae, reporting trouble in the Church
there, and bespeaking the apostle's intervention. So
Paul sat down and wrote a letter to the Church in
Colossae—our *Epistle to the Colossians*—but before he
finished he wrote another little note which we also
possess. It is the Epistle to Philemon, in which Paul
tells Philemon that he is returning his runaway and begs
him to take him back. Thus Onesimus went back to his
old master, and with the best of credentials, an autograph letter from the great apostle.

The Letter

'Paul a prisoner of Christ Jesus and brother Timo-
theus,' the letter begins (Moffatt's translation), 'to our
beloved fellow-worker Philemon, to our sister Apphia
(Philemon's wife), to our fellow-soldier Archippus (possibly their son) and to the Church that meets in your
house: grace and peace to you from God our Father,
and the Lord Jesus Christ.'

Then tactfully Paul paves the way for his main purpose in writing: 'I always thank my God when I mention you in my prayers, for as I hear of your love and
loyalty to the Lord Jesus and to all the saints, I pray
that by their participation in your loyal faith they may
have a vivid sense of how much good we Christians can
attain. I have had great joy and encouragement over
your love, my brother, over the way you have refreshed
the hearts of the saints.'

Evidently, some recent act of hospitality by Philemon
had come to Paul's ears. He alludes to it warmly because he is just about to suggest something that will try

10

Philemon's hospitality to the full. Then, with rare delicacy, he comes to the point:

'Hence although in Christ I would feel quite free to order you to do your duty (mark the note of apostolic authority), I prefer to appeal to you on the ground of love. Well, then, as Paul the old man who nowadays is a prisoner for Christ Jesus, I appeal to you on behalf of my spiritual son, born while I was in prison.'

Thus far we can imagine Philemon reading with pleasure, and, as he comes to the last phrase, speculating who Paul's spiritual son can be. With the next word the secret is out:

'It is Onesimus.' (We need only point out that the name Onesimus means in Greek 'Useful', noting the happy play Paul makes with it.) ' "Useful" was anything but profitable to you in days gone by, but to-day he has become—true to his name—"Right-profitable" —to you—and to me also. I would fain have kept him, for sending him back to you, I feel that I am parting with my own heart. But I did not wish to do anything without your consent. Perhaps this was why you and he were parted for a while, that you might get him back for good, no longer a mere slave, but something more than a slave—a dear brother; especially dear to me, but how much more to you as a man and a Christian.'

Then comes the final appeal: 'You count me a partner? Then receive him as you would receive me. Ah, but perhaps you are still remembering the money he stole? Well, put it down to my account. Look, here is an I.O.U. for the amount: I, PAUL, WILL REPAY. SIGNED BY MY OWN HAND, PAUL. (At this point probably Paul takes the pen in his own hand in order to give his guarantee legal validity.) Come, brother, let me have some return from you in the Lord! Refresh my heart in Christ. I send you this letter relying on your obedience. I know that you will do even more than I tell you.'

Then with a request to get lodgings ready for him— for he hopes soon to be released—Paul sends greetings from all his friends in Rome and ends with a blessing.

Comment on this 'veritable little masterpiece in the art of letter-writing' is hardly necessary. It is a perfect example of Paul's own phrase 'speaking the truth in love'. But two brief observations may fitly round off the chapter.

First, this letter has been styled the *Magna Charta* of the slave. It is not that in it Paul denounces slavery as such; but just as elsewhere he lays it down that 'in Christ there is neither bond nor free', so here in bidding Philemon receive Onesimus not as a slave, but as 'a brother beloved', he enunciates a principle that one day by the grace of God, and the labours of Christian men, was to make an end of that accursed institution.

Second, this letter and the story behind it have been well called 'An Idyll of Grace'. Yes, said Martin Luther, and 'we are all Onesimuses'.

XXI

The Pastoral Epistles

THE Pastoral Epistles, First and Second Timothy and Titus, were so named by Paul Anton of Halle in 1726. The name was apt and stuck, for the letters consist mostly of advice to younger ministers on the defence of the faith, the care of their flocks and their own spiritual life. Their chief aim, apart from denouncing false teaching, is to set up a high standard of Christian character and to urge loyalty to apostolic doctrine.

But was 'the Pastor' Paul? Paul's name certainly stands at the head of each letter; but since the rise of modern Biblical criticism many have doubted his authorship. Nowadays, indeed, the scholars divide themselves into three camps:

Those who accept the full Pauline authorship.
Those who attribute the letters to a follower of Paul's.
Those who think genuine Pauline fragments have been worked up by a disciple of his.

The objections to Paul's authorship are four:

(1) *Historical:* It is urged that the letters cannot be fitted into the historical framework of Paul's life given in Acts. Let the difficulty be granted; yet this objection is not decisive, if only because no man can be sure that Paul's activity ended with the last chapter of Acts. We know from the Prison Letters that Paul hoped to be released from his Roman prison. He had every reason to hope so, for he had done nothing treasonable in the

eyes of the Roman government. As if to confirm this, Eusebius declares that Paul was in fact released, resumed his travelling, and was martyred on his return to Rome. If this be true, we have found a possible place in Paul's life for the Pastoral Epistles.

(2) *Ecclesiastical:* It is urged that the Church in the Pastorals is organized to a degree unknown in Paul's time. This is undoubtedly a first impression: Church polity does seem more advanced; we read of three types of minister—bishops, elders, and deacons; and a roll for widows has been set up, with definite rules and regulations. But, once again, the objection fails to carry complete persuasion. In the Pastorals 'bishops' and 'elders' (as witness Titus 1.5–7) are clearly the same men, 'elder' being their title, 'bishop' describing their function. And we remember that Paul could call the Ephesian elders 'bishops' (Acts 20.17, 28), and that Phil. 1.1 speaks of 'bishops and deacons'.

(3) *Doctrinal:* Here it is urged that the heresies attacked are later than Paul's day and that the letters contain an unpauline stress on 'sound doctrine'. But the heresy denounced is a mixture of Judaism (I Tim. 1.4–7; Titus 1.10; 3.9) and Gnosticism (I Tim. 4.1–5; 6.2 f.). Is this so very different from the Colossian heresy? Once again we must be cautious. Yet, on the purely theological side, we do seem to find unpauline features. For the Pastor, 'faith' often seems equivalent to orthodoxy, and 'righteousness' is predominantly ethical. These things are hardly characteristic of Paul; and what the Pastor has to say about the Law (I Tim. 1.8–11) is certainly not Pauline.

(4) *Stylistic:* Here it is urged that the Pastor's vocabulary and style differ greatly from Paul's. This is perhaps

the weightiest of the objections. For not only does the Pastor use 305 words (out of a total of 897) not found in the admittedly genuine letters of Paul, but his sentences, in their primness and precision, contrast sharply with Paul's rugged and explosive periods. Finally, as P. N. Harrison has emphasized, the Pastor's connecting links and particles differ a good deal from Paul's.

To what conclusion shall we come? The first and second objections are certainly not decisive; but there does seem to be substance in the third and fourth; and if you add them all together, the case against is undoubtedly impressive. Yet who can doubt that, say, in I Tim. 5.23; II Tim. 4.6-22, and Titus 3.12-15 we are listening not to a disciple but to the great apostle himself? Passages like these make the 'hypothesis of fragments' attractive and probable. We may well believe that some genuine notes of Paul to Timothy and Titus fell into the hands of one of his followers, himself a church leader, and that, using them in all good faith, he composed the Pastorals. True, he issued them in Paul's name. But we must not think hardly of him for this— the Pastor was no unscrupulous forger. Did not the letters contain authentic fragments of the great apostle's writing, and did they not give effect to much of his teaching?

The date of the letters as we now have them is probably 90–100.

I Timothy

(Timothy, who had a Jewish mother and a Greek father, became Paul's assistant during his second visit to South Galatia (Acts 16.1 ff.). Thereafter he shared many of Paul's journeys as well as his Roman imprisonment. He has been left in charge of the church at Ephesus.)

Paul to Timothy:

As I urged, stay in Ephesus and oppose these heretics who deal in myths and genealogies. Certain would-be teachers of the Law have renounced sound doctrine and the glorious Gospel which is my trust. (You remember, how I, once a notorious sinner, received Divine mercy.) So I give you this charge (ch. 1):

See that prayers are said for all men. God wishes every man to be saved. (There is only one God, as there is only one mediator, Jesus Christ, who redeemed us all, and whose herald I am.) I desire the men to offer the prayers. The women, who must dress soberly, I do not allow to teach. God created women to bear children, and they will please Him by doing so. (Ch. 2.)

As for bishops, let them be blameless men, married only once, free from avarice, and fit to rule their own households. Recent converts, who may be conceited, should not be chosen. Deacons, too, should be serious, sincere, temperate men, married only once, and to worthy wives.

I hope to come soon; but should I be delayed, this will teach you how to conduct yourself in God's household. (What a wonderful revelation is ours in Christ— manifested, vindicated, preached, exalted!) (Ch. 3.)

Some (we are divinely told) may be led away by teachers of a false asceticism, though we know that everything God made is to be enjoyed. Maintain sound doctrine, keep yourself spiritually fit, and let none despise your youth. Rather, be an example to your people, and cultivate your gift of preaching. (Ch. 4.)

Treat all considerately: young and old, male and female. Widows really alone in the world assist; but if a widow has near relatives, it is their religious duty to care for her. About the Widows' Roll: For enlistment, a widow should be sixty, once married, and well reported for her Christian service. Don't enrol the younger widows—they are likely to be unreliable and slack. Let them marry again and bring up families.

Elders who rule well should be well rewarded, as the scripture says. Never entertain a charge against an elder, unless two or three witnesses support it. Reprimand publicly all errant ones; have no favourites; and never be in a hurry to ordain. (Incidentally, take a little wine, as well as water: it will help your stomach.) (Ch. 5.)

About slaves: They must respect their masters; and should these be Christians, this is no reason why they should respect them less.

Insist on these things. How far from sound doctrine is the conceited 'Gnostic' who loves controversy and thinks religion a source of gain! Religion with contentment is great gain, but money-lust is the ruin of men.

Do you, man of God, fight the good fight, and keep your commission unsullied till Christ's Appearing. Tell the rich to be rich in good deeds—this brings real life. And, for yourself, guard your commission, and avoid this nonsense calling itself 'knowledge'.

Grace be with you. (Ch. 6.)

II Timothy

Paul to Timothy:

I thank God for you and for your Christian nurture, but I urge you to rekindle your ordination gift, and to testify bravely to the Gospel of God's grace in Christ,

whose apostle I am. Though I suffer now, my faith in
His final sufficiency stands firm. Follow the sound teaching I gave you. All in Asia deserted me, but I recall
how faithful, both in Rome and Ephesus, Onesiphorus
was. (May God be merciful to him at the Great Day!)
(Ch. 1.)

Transmit the truth I gave you to reliable men, and be
a loyal soldier of Christ, the Son of David and the Risen
Lord, as my Gospel proclaims. Though I am fettered
now, God's Word is not. Remember the (baptismal)
hymn: 'If we died with him, so shall we live with him.'

Tell your people to avoid the godless talk of the false
teachers. In a great establishment like the Church such
men must needs exist, but keep clear of their silly controversies. (Ch. 2.)

These evils will get worse as the world nears its end;
indeed, some men are already using vile caricatures of
Christianity to ensnare others and serve their own lusts.
You know through what sufferings as an apostle, in
Antioch and Galatia, the Lord sustained me. Christians
must be ready for such suffering. So, in evil times, stay
yourself on your Christian heritage and on Holy Writ
which can equip you as a man of God. (Ch. 3.)

Before God and Christ I charge you to preach the
Word earnestly, and, in the bad times coming when evil
teaching spreads, to do the work of an evangelist. My
time on earth is almost over, as my reward is sure.
Come soon: save for Luke, I am all alone. Bring Mark,
that useful man, and the cloak and books I left at Troas.
Beware of Alexander the coppersmith, a dangerous
man, as I can testify. At my first defence, when all
human helpers failed, the Lord rescued me, as He
always will.

Greet my friends in Ephesus.

Many who fail to see much of the authentic Paul in I Timothy and Titus find him clearly in evidence here. The reference to Lois and Eunice (1.4 f.), the passage beginning, 'I know whom I have believed' (1.12. f.), the paragraph about the 'good soldier of Jesus Christ' (2.1-6), the allusion to 'what befell me at Antioch' (3.10 f.) and practically the whole of the last chapter surely take us behind the Pastor to Paul himself.

Titus

Paul to Titus:

I left you in Crete to amend some defects and to appoint elders in every town. Choose men of integrity, once married, and sound in the faith: good bishops are needed, for many religious charlatans are busy in Crete (resembling the Cretans your prophet described) who profess to know God, yet deny Him by their deeds. These must be silenced. (Ch. 1.)

Teach sound doctrine. Advise the older men to be temperate, and sound in doctrine; the older women, to be reverent, abstemious, and apt to train the younger ones in the domestic virtues. Encourage the younger men to self-control, setting them an example by your life and teaching, and urge the slaves to be obedient and honest. So they will adorn the doctrine of God our Saviour, and we will all live as men redeemed by Christ's sacrifice and waiting for His Appearing. Do this authoritatively. (Ch. 2.)

Remind your people to obey the Civil Powers, avoiding quarrels and showing courtesy. Remember that we too, once hardened sinners, have been saved by God's mercy and justified by His grace. Avoid foolish controversies, and if a man is factious, warn him twice, and then shun him.

Artemas or Tychicus will succeed you in Crete. Do your best to meet me at Nicopolis where I mean to winter.

Greetings from all here, and grace be with you all. (Ch. 3.)

For the clergy the Pastoral Epistles rank among the most valuable in the New Testament, forming as they do a kind of Bible within the Bible which specially belongs to them. Of course, evangelism remains their primary task; but when the converts have been made, there remains the task of grounding them in sound doctrine and wholesome morals. Here the Pastorals are full of wise guidance, as they also have many valuable things to say about the minister's own spiritual life.

Denney once observed that Paul was inspired, but the Pastor was often only orthodox. This is fair comment; but the Pastor's times called for orthodoxy rather than inspiration, and his orthodoxy remains salutary to this day. It is easy to make jokes about 'sound doctrine' and to poke fun at the ultra-orthodox. But in a world like ours where so many unchristian philosophies compete for men's allegiance and so many attempts are made to undermine the Faith, who can deny the need for 'sound doctrine'? If, as we must believe, it is no light thing to 'make shipwreck of the Faith' (I Tim. 1.19), the Pastor's message remains relevant.

Finally, all of us may profit by the Pastor's priceless gift of commonsense. He always keeps close to realities, calls evil things by blunt names, and gives his rules in plain black and white. It may sound banal to tell

Christian men to be sober and Christian women to be chaste; but who will deny that these things need still to be said? In fine, in a world where we cannot all be expert theologians or profound mystics the need remains for a plain, unmystical, straightforward Christianity of the kind the Pastor offers us. Let us be grateful for it.

PART FOUR

THE WRITINGS OF THE OTHER APOSTOLIC MEN

XXII

The Epistle of Priesthood

THE Epistle to the Hebrews is three parts tract and one part letter. It begins, and continues, like a tract—a finely written and closely reasoned tract, whose burden is, 'Hold fast your Christian Faith in the face of all trials' —and it ends like a letter with news and greetings. But the writer does not sign his name to it or supply the name of those to whom he wrote, or tell us in what particular time of stress and strain he was writing; so that we are left to make the best guesses we can.

The Author and his Readers

In our Bible the superscription reads:

THE EPISTLE OF PAUL THE APOSTLE TO THE HEBREWS

But if there is one point on which modern scholars agree, it is that Hebrews is *not* Paul's work. But whose then? 'Who wrote the Epistle to the Hebrews,' said Origen, the great Biblical scholar, in the third century, 'God alone knows.' Sixteen centuries later the secret of its authorship still remains with God. That does not prevent us making 'a scientific guess':

In Acts 18.24 we find this description of Apollos, the co-apostle of Paul and friend of Aquila and Priscilla:

'A certain Jew named Apollos, an Alexandrian by race, an eloquent man, mighty in the scriptures.'

Four things are clear:

Apollos was a Jew (who had become a Christian).
He was an eloquent preacher.
He was an Alexandrian.
He was an expert in the scriptures (i.e. the Old Testament).

Now, these are the very characteristics of the man who wrote Hebrews. For

Our author was almost certainly a Jewish Christian.
His many exhortations betray the preacher.
He interprets Christianity in terms of a Platonic philosophy such as was current in Alexandria (e.g. Philo).
He makes a great display of Old Testament scholarship, often allegorizing as the Alexandrians did.

If then we are to put a name on the title-page of Hebrews, there is no better claimant for the honour (as Luther saw first) than Apollos. And if not Apollos, then, 'spiritually speaking, his twin brother'.

To whom did he write? For centuries it was universally held that the recipients of this 'word of exhortation' (as the writer calls his book) were Jewish Christians, who, under threat of persecution, were in danger of relapsing into Judaism. Recently, however, some scholars have argued that the readers were not Jews after all, but Gentiles, and their peril that of relapsing into irreligion. But this view signally fails to explain why a letter written to Gentiles lapsing into irreligion, should take the form of an elaborate running comparison between Christianity and Judaism; and until the champions of the new view produce better arguments, we may wisely follow tradition.

But if the readers were Jewish Christians, where did they live? The best of many answers is Rome. Not only do we find the Epistle first quoted there (by Clement of Rome), but the solitary clue in the Epistle itself seems to point that way. 'They of Italy salute you' (13.24) is, to be sure, ambiguous. It might mean 'those resident in Italy'; but since a greeting from a whole country is unlikely, the phrase probably refers to Italian Christians abroad who send their greetings home.

The date cannot be much later than A.D. 90; for Clement of Rome could quote from it about 95. It may have been written much earlier. Some, indeed, have argued that it must have been written before the fall of Jerusalem and its Temple in A.D. 70. Otherwise, they say, the writer must certainly have pointed to the destruction of the Temple as a crowning proof from history that God had no further use for it. But this is an argument from silence, and therefore precarious. The references to persecution are too vague to allow us to draw any certain conclusion. A reference to Timothy, who is still apparently in active service, warns us not to put the date too late. Perhaps a date about 80 is likeliest.

The Contents of the Epistle

The writer to the Hebrews has a trick of digressing in order to exhort his readers, so that it is not easy to disentangle the thread of his discourse. But once we have recognized this habit, and bracketed the digressions (as is done below), we can follow the march of his majestic argument more easily. Roughly speaking, the Epistle falls into two parts:

Part I: The Main Argument (1.1–10.18).

After declaring that 'God having of old time spoken unto the fathers in the prophets by divers portions and in divers manners, hath at the end of these days spoken unto us in his Son', the writer proceeds to prove Christ greater than the angels through whom (according to tradition) the Law had been given (chs. 1–2). [But in 2.1-4 he digresses to warn his readers against losing their Christian heritage.] Next, he proves Christ superior to Moses (3.1-6). [Again digressing in 3.7–4.13 to warn them not to fall away or miss the promised 'rest of God'.] He then begins his main theme—the high-priesthood of Christ—and finds the twin qualifications of a high-priest—sympathy and divine appointment—fulfilled in Christ (4.14–5.10). [Once again he turns aside to warn them of the perils of stagnation and relapse, ending on a note of encouragement, 5.11–6.20.] Then, at length, he reaches his main argument, which extends from 7.1 to 10.18.

In chapter 7 Christ is shown to belong to a higher order of priesthood represented not by Aaron, but by that primeval priest, Melchizedek (cf. Gen. 14.18-20, and Psalm 110.4); and the Levitical priesthood is superseded by that of Christ, the ideal high-priest.

In chapter 8 he shows that Christ is not only the ideal high-priest, but that He ministers in an ideal sanctuary, and His ministry constitutes the establishment of a New Covenant between God and man.

In chapter 9 he shows that Christ, as the ideal high-priest, offers the perfect sacrifice for sins; and the argument culminates with the proof not only of the futility of Jewish sacrifices, but of the finality of Christ's sacrifice (10.1-18).

Part II: The Closing Exhortation (10.19–13.25).

After urging his readers to avail themselves of 'the new and living way' consecrated for them by Christ into the Holy of Holies, and warning them of the penalties attached to apostasy, he praises their former constancy in persecution, and reminds them that they stand in the succession of the great heroes of faith (10.19–11.40). Their present suffering, he says, is a proof of God's fatherly discipline, and he draws a powerful contrast between the terrors of the old covenant and the glories of the new (ch. 12). The last chapter begins with some counsels and an appeal to imitate their leaders; goes on to warn them against strange teachings; and ends with a noble doxology and some greetings (ch. 13).

The Message of Hebrews[1]

A picture at Catterick Camp, painted during the European War, shows a signaller lying dead in No-man's-land. He had been sent out to repair a cable

[1] *Note on William Manson's View of Hebrews.*
Since this chapter was written, Professor William Manson has powerfully reinforced the view that the readers were Jewish Christians, and produced a variation of the traditional theory which seems to fit the facts better than any other.
The readers are Jewish Christians in Rome who, threatened with persecution, would fain have shrunk back under the cover of the Jewish religion, a religion permitted by Rome as Christianity was not. Living too much in the Jewish part of their faith, they remained backwardly blind to the true horizons of their Christian calling. By contrast, 'the Author' was a man of the same wide, forward-looking vision as the Stephen of Acts 7. Like him, he had glimpsed the universal significance of

broken by shell-fire. There he lies, cold in death, but
with his task accomplished; for in his stiffening hands
he holds the cable's broken ends together. Beneath the
picture there is one pregnant word: 'Through.'

That is a picture-parable of what our author believed
had been accomplished by the redemptive work of
Christ. Sin had snapped the contact between God and
man. Christ, by His atoning sacrifice, had brought the
broken ends together—had restored the sundered
fellowship between God and man. In his own style of
speech, through Christ's work, man has been enabled to
pass, as Judaism could never help him to pass, from the
world of shadows on earth *through* to the world of
reality in heaven.

For, in the view of the writer, religion means
primarily 'access' to God (functioning through worship),
and it is sin which hinders this access and destroys the
communion with God which is man's highest felicity.
If man is ever to attain it, he must somehow 'get

the Fact of Christ and knew that the Church was called to a
world mission.

On this view many things in the letter become luminous: the
Author's call to the new Exodus (3.7-19) and the pilgrim life
of faith (11); his theological proof that the new means of grace
brought by Christ offer the reality which the old means of grace
could only faintly foreshadow; his warnings against 'shrinking
back' (10.38 f.) and his challenge to them to 'go forth to Jesus
outside the camp, bearing his reproach' (13.13).

The Letter must have been written before the Fall of
Jerusalem in A.D. 70. The Temple seems still to be standing
(8.4; 9.6; 10.1): had it fallen the Author must have pointed to
the fact as proof conclusive that God had no further use for
this focus of the ancient sanctities. Two persecutions are mentioned, one past, and the other impending. The first (10.32 f.) is
the trouble which arose in the Roman synagogues when the
Gospel found an entrance there and the Emperor cleared the
Jews out of the Capital (A.D. 49). The second (12.3 ff.) represents the first moves against the Christians which culminated
in the red martyrdom of A.D. 64. All suggests a date about 63.

through' to God. But how? The ritual of the Jewish Law—the whole system of priest and sanctuary and sacrifice—claimed to be able to take him there. Alas, it could not. It might cleanse the flesh, but it could not cleanse the conscience:

> 'Not all the blood of beasts,
>   On Jewish altars slain,
> Could give the guilty conscience peace,
>   Or wash away the stain.'

Christianity is the perfect and final religion because, through Christ's sacrifice, it secures that 'access to God' which all the religious apparatus of Judaism could only at best shadow forth and symbolize. With Christianity we pass—*ex umbris in veritatem*, 'out of the shadows into the truth'.

That, in essence, is the message of our author; and using the Platonic distinction between the two orders of being—the phenomenal and the real—he works it out in an elaborate running contrast: a contrast between the material and make-believe access provided by the Levitical system, and the spiritual and true access to God, now once-for-all established by the work of Christ upon the Cross. In brief, he shows that Christ is the ideal high-priest who, in offering the ideal sacrifice (that of perfect obedience to God), in the ideal sanctuary, has pioneered for men a living way into the Holiest (which is heaven). So Christians are able, by virtue of

> 'That only offering perfect in His eyes,'

to pass by faith, here and now, into the heavenly sanctuary and to have communion with 'the Father of spirits'.

XXIII

The Epistle of Practice

'GIVE a dog a bad name,' says the proverb, 'and hang him.' Martin Luther once gave the Epistle of St James 'a bad name' and nearly succeeded in hanging it. 'A right strawy Epistle,' he declared, 'with no tang of the Gospel about it.' But whatever else it is, the Epistle of James is not an epistle of straw. Theologically deficient he may be by Luther's standards, yet there is in the New Testament no pithier writer, no man in stronger earnest about the practicalities of the Christian religion than St James.

Who was James?

The answer of the Epistle is: 'James a servant of God and of the Lord Jesus Christ' (1.1). No claim is here made to apostolic authorship. Yet many have liked to think that the Epistle is the work of the James *par excellence* in the New Testament—James the Lord's brother, who disbelieving in Christ during the days of His flesh, was won for the Faith by an appearance to him of the risen Lord (I Cor. 15.7). He rose to pre-eminence in the mother-Church of Jerusalem, and died (according to Josephus) a martyr's death in A.D. 62.

Certainly the Jewish cast of the letter, and its half-dozen or so echoes of the Sermon on the Mount (e.g. 2.5 and 5.12) lend colour to this view. On the other hand, the shyness of the Church to admit it to the Canon, the excellence of the Greek, and the rarity of references to Jesus Himself (two only), make us wonder whether 'James the Just' (as he was called) could possibly be the author. It is probably better to find the writer in some other James, a Jewish Christian, occupying a position of authority in the branch of the Church to which he belonged.

James wrote to 'the twelve tribes which are of the Dispersion' (1.1). That, if taken literally, would refer to Jews scattered throughout the world. More probably it describes the Christian Church as a whole, regarded as the new Israel and the inheritor, in Jesus the Messiah, of the promises made to God's ancient people.

Nor is the date easy to fix. If the author was James the Lord's brother, obviously the letter must have been written before A.D. 62; and the primitive type of church organization implied in it (the church is called 'the synagogue') consorts with this. But the writer's apparent knowledge of First Peter, and of Paul's doctrine of 'justification by faith', make a later date likelier, and any time between A.D. 60 and 100 is possible.

The Epistle has been called 'an ethical scrap-book'; and truly, it is so disconnected, as it stands, that it is the despair of the analyst. James takes a topic of practical religion, and in a few terse sentences drives home his point before passing to another. But it is possible, by a little deft rearrangement[1] of his material, to find five little sermons in it:

Temptation (1.2-8, 12-18).

The Rich Man and the Poor (1.9-11; 5.1-6; 4.8-10, 13-16; 2.1-13).

Faith and Works (1.19-25; 2.14-26; 4.17; 3.13-18; 4.1-7).

[1] This arrangement and the following translations are from J. A. Findlay, *The Way, the Truth, the Life.*

The Use and Abuse of the Tongue (1.26 f.; 3.1-12;
4.11 f.; 5.12).
Patience and Prayer (5.7-11, 13-20).

Three short extracts will show the quality of these
sermons:

Hear James, first, on his favourite theme of faith and
works:

'What is the use, my brethren, if a man say he has
faith, and has nothing to show for it? Can his faith save
him? If a brother or sister have no clothing, or lack
daily food, and one of you says to them: "God bless
you; may you be warned and fed," and does not give
them bodily necessities, what is the use of that? So even
faith, unless it shows itself in deeds, is in the nature of
things dead.' (2.14-17.)

Now hear him attacking oppressive landlords:

'Come now, then, you rich men, weep and howl for
the miseries that are coming upon you. Your wealth is
corrupt, your garments moth-eaten, your silver and gold
rusted through; their rust shall testify against you, and
devour your flesh like fire. You made your money, but
you cannot keep it, for the judgment is upon you. See
the pay of the workers who reaped your fields, the pay
you have withheld from them, is crying out, and the
cries of the reapers have reached the ears of the Lord
of hosts.' (5.1-4.)

Finally, hear James on the Source of all blessings:

'Every kindly charity and every perfect boon comes
down from above, from the Source of all light, with
whom is no summer or winter, no night or day' (1.17 f.).

Pithy, prophetic, practical—these three epithets sum up the Epistle. James writes a pointed style; he sprinkles his page with aphorism and epigram; he delights in the imperative mood; ever and anon he lights up his moralizing with a telling figure or simile; and through all his writing there glows a prophetic passion which stamps him as the Amos of the new covenant.

The style is the man; and what James is driving at, from start to finish, is practice. 'They say and do not,' is the gist of his complaint, as his verdict is: 'Just as a body without breath is dead, so is a creed without works.'

Is James then, at odds with Paul on this issue of faith and works? On the surface, Yes; at bottom, No. For by faith and works they mean different things. The faith on which James comes down like a hammer is mere lip-service to a creed—not the utter trust in a living Person which is the nerve of Christianity according to St Paul. Moreover, by 'works' Paul means 'works of law'; James, the lovely deeds of practical religion. They have different ways of putting things, and they lay the emphasis on different places; but there is no essential contradiction between them. For James would have agreed with Paul that 'faith works through love', as Paul would have agreed with James that 'faith without works is dead'; and both would have agreed that 'the first thing to do with faith is to live by it'.

XXIV

The Epistle of Hope

ROBERT LOUIS STEVENSON somewhere recalls a conversation which he had with a Fifeshire labourer hard at work 'mucking a byre' (*Anglicé*, but inadequately 'cleaning a cowshed'). The talk ran on many things but especially on the aims and ends of life; and as they talked, the labourer let fall a remark which revealed the man: 'Him that has aye something ayont [or, as the English would say, "always something ahead of him"] need never be weary.' That man, whether he knew it or not, had caught the accents of First Peter. It is the epistle of hope, not a wistful hoping for the best, but Christian hope—that lively and confident anticipation of heaven which rests on the God who raised Christ from the dead, and gave Him glory that our 'faith and hope might be in him'. It was to keep the lamp of that hope burning brightly in Christian hearts during dark days that Peter wrote his Epistle. But what dark days were these, and who were the readers who needed this recall to Christian hope?

The Author and his Readers

Before we discuss the readers, let us say a few words about the author.

'Peter an apostle of Jesus Christ'—the Epistle begins. Near the end, in a sort of postscript, we read: 'By Silvanus . . . I have written unto you.' The letter purports to have been written by the Apostle Peter with Silvanus,

Paul's old comrade, as his amanuensis. Moreover, tradition is all in favour of this claim; for all the Church Fathers ascribe the Epistle to the apostle. Furthermore, the contents of the letter itself, so far as they go (see especially 1.8; 5.1, 5) seem to corroborate the tradition.

Yet, like most things in the New Testament, the apostolic authorship of First Peter has been challenged.

First, it is asked: Could a Galilean fisherman have written the tolerably good Greek of this Epistle? One feels almost inclined to retort: could a Bedford tinker have written *The Pilgrim's Progress*? But there is no need; for the good Greek of the letter can easily and naturally be credited to Silvanus: 'the voice may well be Peters' voice, though the literary hand may have been the hand of Silvanus'.[1]

Next, it is said that this letter contains too many echoes of St Paul's Epistles to be the authentic work of St Peter. We may candidly admit that there are similarities; but when we remember how much of what used to be vaguely styled 'Paulinism' is now shown to be common apostolic Christianity, and, further, that Silvanus had been a close friend of Paul's, we must judge this an insufficient reason for denying the Petrine authorship.

Finally, it is urged that the references to persecution in First Peter imply a time when it was illegal to be a Christian, i.e. in the time of Pliny *c.* A.D. 112, when, presumably, Peter was dead. But this is to read too much into the references. They imply no more than widespread popular suspicion and hostility. We do well to remember that it is still possible to counsel loyalty to the state (2.13-17). In short, a time just before Nero's

[1] A. H. MacNeile, *N.T. Teaching in the Light of St Paul's*, p. 136.

outburst, say 63–4, would fit the implied facts of the
Epistle.

So, with most British scholars, we may attribute the
letter to St Peter, adding only that Silvanus was probably more than a mere amanuensis.

Peter's readers were, in his own words, 'the elect who
are sojourners of the Dispersion, in Pontus, Galatia,
Cappadocia, Asia and Bithynia'. At first blush, that
might suggest Jews in Asia Minor; but the contents of
the Epistle show that the readers were largely Gentiles,
and there can be little doubt that the words describe the
Christians in Asia Minor who form part of the true
People of God scattered abroad in an alien world.

Where was the Epistle written? The clue is to be
found in I Peter 5.13: 'She that is in Babylon elect together with you saluteth you.' 'She' might be Peter's
wife, or even some early Countess of Huntingdon! But
scholars are fairly agreed that 'she' means the local
church from which St Peter writes. 'Your sister church
in Babylon', Moffatt boldly translates. But Babylon?
Can this be the once famous city on the Euphrates?
That is just possible; but practically every scholar of
repute nowadays takes Babylon here to be, as it is in
Revelation, a cryptic name for Rome.

The date, as suggested above, must be about A.D. 64.

The Letter

A short paraphrase of the letter will best suggest its
contents. After his opening address, Peter breaks out
into a noble recital of the *blessings* of God's redeemed
children:

'Blessed be God who through Christ's resurrection
has kindled in our hearts a living hope of a heavenly

inheritance! Present trials, bravely endured, will prove
the quality of your faith and, at last, end in glory. Long
ago prophets discerned afar off the salvation now become yours in Christ. So, remembering how costly was
your redemption, live holy lives and love one another
heartily. As newborn children of God, be done with evil,
and grow up into that spiritual house of which Christ is
the corner-stone. Yes, Christ is "the Stone" described in
prophecy which has proved a stumbling-block to some.
But you who believe in Him, are God's true People,
called from darkness into His marvellous light.' (1.3–
2.10.)

Then Peter passes to their *duties* as Christians in the
world:

'Let your pure lives confute your pagan critics. Submit to the authorities, and as God's free men, honour
all. Servants should obey their masters, even if it means
suffering unjustly, for they follow in the steps of the
Servant-Son of God whose stripes have proved their
healing. Wives should submit to their husbands. It is
not outward adorning but the inner beauty of a gentle
spirit that pleases God. (Remember the holy women of
old.) Husbands should treat their wives chivalrously,
and all should be sympathetic and forgiving. Blessed are
those who suffer for the right's sake! Make Christ Lord
in your hearts, and be quick to reply to those who ask
a reason for your Christian hope. Let your pure conscience shame your libellers. So you will copy Christ
who died for sins, and went and preached to the spirits
in prison.[1] The saving of Noah's household by water in
the antediluvian days has now its counterpart in Bap-

---

[1] The N.T. basis for the 'He descended into Hell' (i.e. Sheol)
clause in the Apostles' Creed.

tism. Let your life be given to the doing of God's will. Once, before your conversion, you lived like profligates; and now your pagan neighbours, expecting you still so to behave, revile you when you refuse. Never mind; they will have to answer to God who shall judge both living and dead (that is why the Gospel had to be preached to the dead). The end is near: be calm and prayerful: love and serve all. Whatever your gift, use it as servants of God and to his glory.' (2.11–4.11.)

Finally, Peter deals with their *trials* in the world:

'Your impending ordeal should not surprise you, who know that Christ also had to suffer. As you share in this suffering, rejoice. Let none suffer as evil-doers; and if you have to suffer as Christians, glorify God for it. Judgment is beginning; and if it starts with God's family, what will be the fate of unbelievers? I, Peter, your co-presbyter and witness of Christ's sufferings, charge you to shepherd God's flock faithfully, and the Chief Shepherd will reward you. Be humble—so God will exalt you; be watchful—the devil is abroad; and be ready to pay the same tax of suffering as your brothers in the world. When your suffering is past, God will strengthen you.' (4.12–5.11.)

So, with a commendation of Silvanus 'the trusty brother', and a greeting from the local church, and 'Mark my son', Peter concludes: 'Peace be to you all who are in Christ Jesus.'

'Blessed are they,' said Jesus, 'that have been persecuted for righteousness' sake: for theirs is the kingdom of heaven.' There is no better commentary on the beatitude than this Epistle. Here is no 'grey and close-lipped Stoicism' which can only 'grin and bear it'; here is a document which has caught the authentic spirit of that

Master 'who for the joy that was set before him endured
the Cross', which though the skies lower and the enemy
press hard and heavy, glows with that hope, that
buoyant expectancy, of 'an inheritance incorruptible
and undefiled and that fadeth not away', eternal in the
heavens.[1]

[1] *Note on I Peter (as a Baptismal Homily).*
Some modern scholars, who cannot believe that Peter wrote
this letter and date it late, tell us that we should see in it a
baptismal homily (1.3–4.11) which has been combined with
another letter to a persecuted community (4.12–5.11).
The weaknesses of this theory are these:
(1) It arbitrarily dismisses as late fictions the opening saluta-
tions and the *personalia* at the end.
(2) It makes a complete break between 1.3–4.11 and 4.12–5.11,
though the sufferings of 1.6 are surely those of 4.12.
(3) It forces baptismal meanings on quite general passages.

XXV

The Correspondence of the Elder

I John

IF, among the Catholic Epistles, Hebrews is the Epistle of Priesthood, James the Epistle of Practice, and First Peter the Epistle of Hope, the First Epistle of St John is the Epistle of Life. For St John, 'life' or 'eternal life' is a synonym for salvation—the salvation of which God in Christ is the source. (To have eternal life is for John the equivalent of 'being in the Kingdom' (the Synoptic Gospels) and of 'being in Christ' (St Paul).) With 'life' John begins (1.1), and with 'life' he ends (5.20). If we ask what he means by 'life', the reply is: the life which is life indeed, life lived in fellowship with God, and His Son Jesus Christ, life freed from the dominion of sin, life whose finest fruit is love, life that can never die

The Author, his Aim, and his Readers

Though the Epistle is anonymous, the author was clearly some venerable father in God, whose ripe Christian experience enabled him to write this charming pastoral letter to his 'little children'. Who was he? If style and thought prove anything, the Epistle is by the same hand as the Fourth Gospel. Not only do we find in the Epistle the same distinctive idioms and phrases, but there is hardly a thought in the Epistle which does not find its parallel in the Gospel; and the same great contrasts of light and darkness, good and evil, love and hate, life and death, pervade the Epistle no less profoundly than they do the Gospel. First John is therefore, in all probability, the work of John the Elder, the disciple of the Apostle John. (We note that in II and III John, which are almost certainly by the same hand, the author calls himself 'The Elder'.) The place of writing then will be the same: Ephesus or its neighbourhood; the readers will be the local churches in the 'diocese' of Ephesus; and the date, like that of the Gospel, will be in the last decade of the first century. Though no certainty is possible, it is an attractive conjecture that the Epistle was written as a postscript to the Gospel; the Gospel being written to explain how men might have eternal life (John 20.31), and the Epistle to explain how they might know that they had it (I John 5.13).

St John wrote primarily to build up his readers in the Christian faith. But he had another aim. Paradoxically, this Epistle whose master-word is love is also strongly polemical. If its first aim is to edify, its second aim is to attack—to attack the 'spirit of error'. The error was Docetism—Docetism of a 'Cerinthian' brand. Docetism was an early heresy which denied the human nature of Christ, averring that His body was only a semblance. Among the Docetists was a man called Cerinthus who lived in and around Ephesus near the end of the first century. According to him, Jesus and Christ were two separate beings, Christ being a celestial power, or 'aeon', who descended on Jesus at His Baptism and left Him before the Crucifixion. This was, in effect, a denial of the doctrine of the Incarnation, and its practical consequences seem to have been, firstly, a denial of the reality of sin and, secondly, a loveless intellectualism.

If we read the Epistle carefully, we shall catch the undertones of John's controversy with the Cerinthians.

Whenever he begins a sentence with, 'If we say . . .' 'If anyone says . . .'; or strongly affirms that Jesus is the Son of God; or pillories the man who, professing to love God, hates his brother, we may be sure that John has Cerinthus, or his like, in his eye. And yet the Epistle is very far from being all polemics; for time and time again John lifts the whole matter out of the dust of mere polemics into the lucid atmosphere of eternal truth:

The Plan of the Epistle

At first reading the Epistle appears plan-less—a collection of meditations 'spiralling'[1] round a few main themes. On closer study, we see that it is really an apparatus of tests for the possession of eternal life, based upon three great conceptions of God. 'The Epistle divides itself into three main sections, introduced—the second not very clearly at 2.25—by definitions of God. God is light (1.5). God is life (2.25). God is love (4.8). And the question investigated under each head is, Are we walking in the light? Are we begotten of God? Are we dwelling in love? And three tests are proposed under each section, the tests of right living, genuine loving, and true believing.'[2]

So we may analyse the epistle thus:

Prologue. Eternal life made manifest in Jesus (1.1-4).

God is Light. Do we walk in the light? Then we must
Live in the light, and walk as He walked. (Right living: 1.5–2.6.)
Love our brother—and not the world. (Genuine loving: 2.7-17.)

[1] 'Spiral' is the word that best describes John's type of thought. See Law, *The Tests of Life*, p. 5.
[2] J. A. Robertson, in Weymouth's Translation of the New Testament.

Believe that Jesus is the Christ, the Son of God. (True believing: 2.18-24.)

God is Life. Are we children of the living God? Then we must

Do righteousness, as His children. (Right living: 2.25–3.10.)

Love one another . . . in deed and truth. (Genuine loving: 3.11-18.)

Confess that Jesus Christ is come in the flesh. (True believing: 3.19–4.6.)

God is Love. Do we dwell in love? Then we must (here the tests melt into 'love')

Love one another.

Do His commandments.

Believe that Jesus is the Christ who came by water and blood (4.7–5.12).

Epilogue. The assurance of eternal life. Prayer for ourselves and others. The threefold 'we know' (5.13-21).

The Value of the Epistle

Even polemics, under the providence of God, yield their happy fruits. For the twin glories of this Epistle are, firstly, its emphasis on the Incarnation and, secondly, its emphasis on love.

The core of the Christian doctrine of the Incarnation is that 'God was in Christ'—that in Jesus, who was 'born of the Virgin Mary, suffered under Pontius Pilate', the transcendent God stooped low for us men and our salvation. Cerinthus and his friends, by reducing the Incarnation to a mere semblance, drove John to reaffirm its reality with all the spiritual passion at his command. To all their speculations he replies uncompromisingly: 'Jesus Christ is come in the flesh.' 'Whosoever denieth the Son, the same hath not the Father. He that confesseth the Son hath the Father also.' Of course St John was right. If God was not really 'in Christ', the Gospel is 'a tale told by an idiot, full of sound and fury, signifying nothing'. The Incarnation is 'the roof and crown' of all Christian truth.

The other glory of the Epistle is its magnificent insistence on the primacy of love in the Christian life. No less than fifty-two times does John use the word 'love', or others of the same meaning. Time and time again he insists that 'only love is true churchmanship'. And this is really only the practical corollary of his doctrine of God in Christ. It is because love is the law of God's being, supremely evidenced in the sending of Christ His Son, that we must love our brethren, and by so loving show the reality of our Christian sonship. 'Beloved, if God so loved us, we also ought to love one another.' Cf. 4.7-11.

Yet, as Carlyle says, 'there is nothing inexorable but love'; and though John never tires of saying, 'Little children, love one another', he blazes out indignantly at that pseudo-Christianity which, feigning love for God, looks with loveless eyes upon its Christian brethren: 'If a man say, I love God, and hateth his brother, he is a liar: for he that loveth not his brother whom he hath seen, cannot love God whom he hath not seen' (4.20). Of St John, then, we may fitly say (in Browning's words):

'Like Dante, he loved well, because he hated—
Hated wickedness, and all that hinders loving.'

II John

Imagine a venerable 'bishop' who, hearing of the spread of false doctrine in his diocese, writes a pastoral letter about the danger, and then learning of a particular church being badly affected, decides to send it a brief note containing the gist of his previous letter. This we take to be the relation between I and II John.[1] II John is a miniature of I John, with hardly a phrase not found in the bigger letter; and its author, 'the Elder', must be the same, John the Elder of Ephesus. That 'the elect lady' named in the first verse is a church, not a woman, seems certain (cf. I Peter 5.13. 'The children of thine elect sister salute thee' (v. 13) is a greeting from the Elder's church.)

Evidently some members of the church addressed, on a visit to the Elder, had given him a report which both pleased and vexed him. He was pleased that certain faithful folk stood by the truth and walked in love (4–6). What vexed him was the news of the spread of an 'advanced' doctrine which, in effect, denied the reality of the Incarnation.[2] In his reply (7–11), which paves the way for a personal visit (12), he declares that any 'advanced doctrine' which severs itself from the historic Christian faith is delusive—lose the true doctrine of Jesus as the Son, and you lose the Father too—and he bids them boycott the heretics. 'Shut your doors on them,' is the burden of his advice, 'and cut them in the street.' Drastic measures indeed, which seem at variance

---

[1] Streeter (*The Primitive Church*, pp. 83–89) argues persuasively that the Elder was in fact bishop of Ephesus, the mother-Church of Asia, exercising a position and a responsibility for the smaller churches of the province which made him practically an 'Archbishop'.

[2] As in I John, the heretics were obviously 'Docetists'.

with the Christian law of love! To this the Elder might have retorted that in face of the perilous situation no toleration was possible. 'Love,' Reinhold Niebuhr has observed, 'is always relevant but never a simple possibility.' In a situation like this, the problem (and it is ours as well as the Elder's) is to find a way of living with those who differ *toto caelo* from us theologically, a way which neither infringes the Christian law of love nor compromises our loyalty to the truth.

III John

III John, probably written by 'the Elder' from Ephesus about the same time as I and II John (i.e. 90–100), might be called 'the Johannine Philemon', because it is a private note concerned with personal relations. Yet, as in Philemon, there is a local church in the background—perhaps the very church to which II John was sent. (In that case, III John 9 refers to II John.)

It was a 'row' in the church which evoked the letter, and the chief persons concerned in it were:

The Elder, who wrote the letter;
Gaius, who received it;
Diotrephes, whose action provoked it; and
Demetrius, who carried it.

Diotrephes who held the chief office in the church (and 'loved his pre-eminence,' comments the Elder grimly) evidently resented any 'direction' from the Elder in Ephesus. Not only had he refused to receive some missioners whom the Elder had sent to him, but he had even excommunicated local church members who gave them hospitality. So, in this letter, the Elder writes to his friend Gaius (perhaps the minority leader), thanking him for past kindness to the missioners and asking his support for them on their second visit (2–8). He hopes himself to come soon and to bring Diotrephes to his senses. Then, after commending Demetrius who is to carry the letter (and may have been the leader of the missionaries), he sends greetings.

What may we learn from III John? That church leaders with 'diotrephic' tendencies are dangerous? Yes; but, as Streeter observed,[1] 'one cannot be a "Jack in office", unless the office is already there.' Diotrephes not only loved the chief place in his local church—he actually held it, and exercised his powers to the discomfiture of others. The conclusion is hard to resist that Diotrephes was the first known representative of 'monarchical episcopacy'. Here is something of much significance for the church historian.

[1] *The Primitive Church*, p. 85.

XXVI

Contending for the Faith

WHO was Jude? If he was 'the brother of James' (1), he was the Jude of Mark 6.3 and 'Founder's kin'. (The grandsons of this Jude were leaders in the churches and lived until Trajan's reign.) Certainly his knowledge of the Old Testament and the book of Enoch[1] (14 f.) suggests a Jew. If he was another Jude, Streeter's guess that he was Jude, the third bishop of Jerusalem, is as good as any. Where his readers lived is a matter of conjecture —possibly in Syrian Antioch. Take the writer to be the brother of James, and a date for the letter later than 70–80 is unlikely. If he was another Jude, it may belong to the end of the first century.

But we do know why he wrote. He was 'contending for the faith once for all delivered to the saints' (3). Heretics were menacing the loyalty of the faithful. These men were apparently Christian libertines (4) who by their unbelief, irreverence, insubordination, carousing and immorality were disgracing the fair name they bore. It is no part of a Christian's duty to call people by soft names when they merit hard ones. In this spirit Jude denounces the heretics. First, however, he holds out before his readers, as 'an awful warning', the fate which overtook the disobedient Israelites in the Wilderness, the rebellious angels, the Cities of the Plain. Then

---

[1] The reference in v.9 to Michael disputing with the devil for the body of Moses comes from the pseudepigraphic *Assumption of Moses*.

he turns on the trouble-makers. 'They are blemishes on your love feasts,' he says, 'as they boldly carouse together, looking after themselves.' And his anger blazes into magniloquence: 'Waterless clouds . . . fruitless trees . . . wild waves, casting up the foam of their own shame, wandering stars for whom the nether gloom of darkness has been reserved.' (12 f.)

But when he has emptied the vials of his vituperation on the heretics, the denunciations give place to a series of noble imperatives:

'But you, beloved, build yourselves up on your most holy faith; pray in the Holy Spirit; keep yourselves in the love of God; wait for the mercy of our Lord Jesus Christ unto eternal life. And convince some who doubt; save some, by snatching them out of the fire; on some have mercy with fear, hating even the garment spotted by the flesh.' (19–22.)

And in a noble closing doxology he lifts his readers into the heavenly places. (24 f.)

Some men deserve to live in history by virtue of a single phrase. Jude is one of them. The man who said, 'Keep yourselves in the love of God,' surely deserves a place, however humble, in the Canon.

XXVII

The Promise of His Coming

WE have separated II Peter from I Peter and put it after Jude for three good reasons: (1) It is almost certainly not Peter's work, (2) it borrows freely from Jude, and (3) it is the latest book in the New Testament.

Here are five reasons why Peter cannot have written the letter. First, early Church Fathers like Origen and Eusebius had grave suspicions about it. Second, in tone and substance it bears no kind of resemblance to I Peter. Third, its rather baroque Greek was surely never written by a Galilean fisherman. Fourth, it borrows wholesale from Jude.[1] Fifth, it refers to Paul's letters as 'scripture' (3.16). Considerations like these compel every candid scholar to refuse the letter to Peter and to ascribe it to some church leader who, about the middle of the second century, borrowed the authority of Peter's great name to enforce his warning to his readers.

Our author was worried by the activity of false teachers in his community. That they were libertines is clear enough; but it was their scoffing attitude to the hope of Christ's Second Advent which mainly moved him to write. They were saying to the faithful: 'Where is the promise of his Coming? Generation after generation has gone by, and still he has not come. Let us abandon this foolish expectation.' To these men our author has an answer which we shall consider presently.

The letter itself consists of a 'Be zealous', a 'Beware', and a 'Be prepared'. First, calling himself 'an eye-

[1] II Peter 2.1–3.3 shows at least a dozen borrowings from Jude 4–18.

witness of his majesty' (the Transfiguration) and re-
minding them of the sure word of prophecy, he bids
them be zealous to 'make their calling and election
sure'. (Ch. 1.) Next, borrowing most of Jude's 'sanctions', he tells his readers to beware of the heretics.
'They promise you freedom,' he warns, 'but they themselves are slaves of corruption.' (Ch. 2.) Then, rounding
on the scoffers, he declares the coming of the Day of the
Lord to be certain, and bids them follow the advice of
'our beloved brother Paul' and prepare for it by growing in the grace and knowledge of the Saviour. (Ch. 3.)

Should we have been the poorer if the Church, en-
dorsing the suspicions of its leaders, had excluded II
Peter from the Canon? Perhaps not. Yet we should have
lost a lovely sentence like 'until the day dawns and the
morning star rises in your hearts' (1.19), a wry comment
on Paul's letters (3.15 f.), and, above all, a wise word
about Christ's Coming. We may, or we may not, believe
that the world is destined to go up in flames 'with a
loud noise' (though our scientists would hardly dismiss
the possibility); but, like 'Peter', we must believe that
one day God is going to 'wind up' history and make a
final end of evil. So we may find a salutary message still
in what he says to the scoffers: 'With the Lord one day
is as a thousand years, and a thousand years as one day.
The Lord is not slow about his promise as some count
slowness, but is forbearing toward you, not wishing that
any should perish, but that all should reach repentance.'
(3.8 f.) Till the Day of the Lord comes, it is our duty to
'make our calling and election sure' while 'according to
his promise we wait for new heavens and a new earth
in which righteousness dwells'. (3.13.)

This is surely well said, and was worth saying.

XXVIII

The Judgment and Victory of God

WHEN we pass from the other books of the New Testament to the Revelation of St John the Divine, our feeling is that of men who cross from some familiar terrain into an alien and uncanny land. Revelation is, to our modern mind, a very weird and fantastic book full of angels and trumpets and earthquakes, of beasts and dragons and demons of the pit. We are not at all surprised to learn that the early Church hesitated long about including it in the Canon: it puzzles us as it puzzled them. And yet we may be glad that they finally plumped for its inclusion; for it makes a glorious ending to the New Testament. The Gospels tell how in the fullness of time Jesus brought God's promised salvation to men. The book of Acts relates how the apostles brought the Good News of it from Jerusalem to Rome. The Epistles apply its truths to the multifarious problems of everyday life in the world. But there is one note in the 'new song' of salvation still to be heard in its fullness, and Revelation supplies it. For the final note is from the trumpets of heaven, and the New Testament ends with a 'Hallelujah Chorus'—with the sound of the great multitude of the redeemed singing their songs of redemption in the presence of God and the Lamb.

Concerning Apocalypses

Scholars call this book 'The Apocalypse'. The word is simply Greek for 'unveiling'; and Revelation is the finest Christian example of what is known as 'apocalyptic literature', that is, writings which purport to 'unveil' the Last Things, to give us visions of the end of the world, and of the final judgment and victory of God.

Our book, then, is no Melchizedek in the world of letters; it had literary ancestors not a few. To be sure, the Bible contains only one other writing of the same literary *genre*, Daniel; but in the years 200 B.C.–A.D. 100 the Jews produced many such books. They soon fell, however, into disrepute and were gradually forgotten, so that it is only in recent times we have rediscovered many of them. In fact, we now possess, in whole or in part, about thirty apocalypses, and a study of them has enormously increased our understanding of Revelation.

Apocalyptic literature is mostly the fruit of persecution. When evil forces seem supreme in the world and religious people are suffering for their loyalty to God and His laws, they inevitably fly for comfort to things unseen, to their sure hope that the Judge of all the earth will yet do right by punishing the wicked and vindicating His saints. What more natural than that men who, in their misery still hold fast their faith in God, should dream dreams and see visions of that blessed vindication. These visions, when they are set down in writing, we call apocalypses. If we ask why their language should be so cryptic and fantastically symbolic, at least two reasons can be given. For one thing, these books attempt to utter the unutterable—to peer into the future and the unseen world; and it is only in the language of symbol that man can do that. But, more important, these apocalypses carry a dangerous message and are born in a time when freedom of speech is in eclipse. Your apocalyptic writer dare not deal in plain speech; he must wrap his message up in a sort of cipher language to which (he hopes) only his readers will have the key. That is also partly the reason why apocalyptic writers, instead of signing their own names to their works, generally father them on some great worthy of the past like Daniel or Enoch.

The Author of Revelation and his Readers

Our author, however, is an exception to this last rule. We know at least that his name was John. That he was not John the Fourth Evangelist seems as certain as anything in criticism: in both manner and matter (as Dionysius saw long ago) the two books are poles apart. But if not he, then who? All we can say is that he must have been a leader in the churches of Asia, that he had been exiled for his religion to the lonely isle of Patmos in the Aegean Sea (a Roman State prison), and—this from his style—that he must have been a Jewish Christian. We may distinguish him from John the Evangelist by calling him 'John the Seer'.

For whom did he write and when?

It is a far cry from the Christians in Germany under the Third Reich to the Christians of Asia Minor under the Roman Empire in the first century A.D. But one thing is common to both—persecution for the Faith. As the Christians in Germany were persecuted by the Nazis because they would not swear undivided allegiance to Hitler, so the Christians of Asia Minor eighteen centuries ago were persecuted by the Roman government because they refused to bow the knee to Caesar.

The suffering people for whom John wrote were the Christians in the seven churches of Ephesus, Smyrna, Pergamum, Thyatira, Sardis, Philadelphia and Laodicea. In A.D. 64 (as we saw) the persecution of the Church by

Nero had begun. Thirty years later, under the Emperor Domitian, the smouldering fires blazed out again. The excuse for persecution can be put in two words: emperor worship. Earlier emperors had done something to encourage this cult in the hope of producing a sort of state religion which would unify the empire. Domitian, however, enforced it in strong earnest, and began in Asia Minor. Statues of the emperor were set up, priests appointed, and the subject peoples ordered to accord divine honours to the emperor.

This was, of course, a very serious business for sincere Christians. To One only could divine honours be paid; and yet to disobey the imperial edict was to court exile and death. It was to Christians in this desperate dilemma that John the Seer wrote his book. Irenaeus tells us that he wrote near the end of Domitian's reign (about A.D. 96), and the whole tenor of the book confirms this. And John wrote with a very practical purpose —to fortify his fellow Christians to stand fast in the face of this threat, assured that God would deliver and vindicate His saints.

His book takes the form of a letter (see its beginning and end), and was meant to be read in church. But it is best regarded as a great drama of divine judgment and victory in which the action moves inexorably forward, in scene after scene, to its ending. For the material of these scenes John has drawn on many sources: his own visions, Christian apocalyptic utterances, like Mark 13, the Old Testament, Jewish apocalyptic books, and even pagan myths. But all are skilfully woven into a whole, and the drama flames to its great climax in the destruction of Babylon, which is Rome, and the vindication of God's People, which is the Christian Church.

Contents of Revelation

Prologue (ch. 1)

John, exiled in Patmos, salutes the Seven Churches in Asia, and tells how the heavenly Christ granted him the visions of impending events which he will now relate.

Messages to the Seven Churches (chs. 2–3)

These take the form of letters dictated by Christ to John, and addressed to the Seven Churches. Smyrna and Philadelphia receive praise; Ephesus, Pergamum and Thyatira, praise mixed with censure; Sardis, stern rebuke; and Laodicea, condemnation. The burden of all the letters is that a fearful crisis overhangs the churches. Christ will deliver His saints, but only if their loyalty is worthy of Him.

The Vision of Heaven (chs. 4–5)

Now the revelation proper begins. Through an open door in heaven John beholds the ineffable God on His throne adored by the heavenly hosts (including four and twenty Elders, the representatives of the Old and New Israels). God hands the scroll of Judgment to Christ, who alone is found worthy to undo its seals.

The Coming of the Woes (chs. 6–11)

Heralded by the breaking of seals and the peal of trumpets, the divine 'woes' now fall thick and fast on the earth. Angelic emissaries go forth to send war, pestilence, and famine on the world. Still more terrible grow these calamities till the whole earth is made desolate. (Yet the picture is not one of unrelieved horror, for ever and anon there occur interludes in which we are allowed to hear the songs of the redeemed, or to glimpse the glories of heaven.)

The Appearance of the Beast (chs. 12–16)

With the Story of the Woman and the Child (the Messiah) attacked by the Dragon, we are now reminded that the present crisis is but a phase of an agelong struggle between God and Satan who, cast down from heaven, renews his evil work on earth. His tool is a seven-headed Beast, unmistakably the Roman Empire. One of the heads of the Beast—a Roman Emperor— goes down into the Abyss, and rises in the shape of Antichrist, to war on the People of God. (A smaller beast represents the priesthood of the Caesar-cult in Asia Minor.) Then one angel after another proclaims doom on the Beast and Babylon, and the harvest of judgment begins. The seven bowls of God's wrath, full of plagues, are poured on earth; battle is joined between God and Satan; and fearful portents prelude the ruin of Babylon.

The Fall of Rome (chs. 16–19)

The fall of Rome (pictured as a harlot, drunk with the blood of the saints) is now related in a grimly magnificent passage, and the resultant paeans in heaven have hardly died away when Christ rides forth with an angelic army to vanquish the Beast and his worshippers.

The Consummation (chs. 20–22.5)

When Christ has conquered His enemies (we are told), He will first initiate a reign of bliss on earth for His saints which will last a thousand years. Then the Devil, who has meanwhile lain bound in prison, will escape to make his last onset on God's people. When he is finally overthrown, the earthly paradise will yield to an eternal kingdom of God in which all His purposes will be consummated.

The Epilogue (22.6-21)

In his closing words, John tells his readers that these things will happen soon: Christ will return to claim His Bride, which is the Church. So, with a curse on all who tamper with his book, John writes a benediction.

The Interpretation and Value of the Book

No book of the New Testament has suffered more at the hands of ill-instructed interpreters than this. Of many errors of interpretation two have been fraught with much harm. One is to regard it as a sort of Christian Sibylline Oracles full of cryptic allusions to far-distant events and people. The other is to interpret the book with a crude literalism, and to invest the incidents in it with an occult significance. Thus, to take one example only, in chapter 13.18, we read of a Beast-man whose number is 666. This is not the Pope or Napoleon, or even Hitler. In the opinion of the best scholars, it is Nero, or rather Nero *redivivus*; for John evidently adopted a current belief that Nero, who had been dead thirty years, was destined to rise and return with an army as Antichrist incarnate. Therefore, it cannot be insisted on too strongly that the book must be read in the light of the times when it was written, and the allusions sought in the people and events of that age. Again, the man who would read Revelation intelligently must familiarize himself with the symbolic language of apocalyptic. Angels and beasts and weird monsters are its conventional stock in trade. As for the mystic numbers, if we remember that three is the number of heaven, four the number of earth, and seven the number of per-fection, we have a key to the odd arithmetic of Revelation. But perhaps the best advice we can give is that the reader study this book with the help of a scholar who knows the true nature of apocalyptic, and who, resisting the temptation to lose himself in details, aims to set torth the broad meaning and purpose of the book. (Here E. F. Scott's *The Book of Revelation* (SCM Press) may be strongly recommended.)

If Revelation belongs to the first century, it may be asked what value it can possibly have for us. What Word of God for our day are we to find in the distem-pered dreams of a first-century apocalyptist who, in point of fact, did not accurately prognosticate the course of future history even in his own day?

First and foremost, Revelation is 'a message for a crisis'. In times of peace and prosperity it will have few readers; but when a great crisis in history arises, as it has arisen in our time, and with evil unmasked and rampant in the earth, the hearts even of the strongest begin to fail them for fear, then Revelation becomes astonishingly relevant, and the truths behind its vivid imagery leap out on us like flashes of lightning. For the message of John the Seer is that, through all this horror of evil, God is working out His great purpose of judg-ment and redemption, and the cause of God's faithful People will not be suffered to fail in the world. So re-garded, Revelation is a trumpet-call to faith in a time of chaos and catastrophe.

Which brings us to the second main lesson of Revela-tion. Behind and beneath the apocalyptic *bizarrerie* of the book there is a noble expression of eternal principles —those great principles of God's government of the

13

world traceable in every era of the world's history. Put in simple terms, the message of Revelation is that good in this world is continually beset by evil. For different people, at different times this conflict becomes almost intolerable. To such Revelation comes with the reminder that they are not left to fight the battle alone, that they have unseen allies, that a righteous God governs the world, that in the end all evil must be destroyed, and that 'the faith and patience of the saints' will be rewarded, if not in this world, then in the next.

And this brings us to the last aspect of the book's permanent value, which is its invincible conviction of the reality of the unseen world. Throughout his book John sets the two worlds continually over against each other—the heavenly world in its beatitude and glory, and the earthly one convulsed and collapsing in evil. So sure is he of that higher world that in every age when God's servants are tempted in face of the giant power of evil to lose heart and faith, John's book has power to infect them with his own certitude of the heavenly world. Thus it is (as someone has said) that Revelation, beyond all other books, has made people feel that heaven is real; and in the strength of that blessed conviction go forth anew to do battle with the world and all its evils.

EPILOGUE

The Unity of the New Testament

WE have now considered how the New Testament came
into being, and passed in review its chief books, as
modern scholarship sees them. From a literary angle, it
has been a study in variety. In plain language, the New
Testament is a literary hotch-potch: here are all sorts of
literary forms and specimens: first, four books called
'Gospels' like biographies in some respects, in others
quite unlike; then a volume of history; then a very
mixed epistolary bag; and finally a specimen of apocalyptic writing. The diversity, however, does not end
there: it extends to subject-matter. For when we study
the contents of the various books, our first impression
may well be that the writers are all discussing different
things. To take one example only, the dominant theme
of the Synoptic Gospels seems to be 'the Kingdom (or
Reign) of God'; of St Paul's Epistles 'being in Christ' (a
phrase that occurs more than a hundred and fifty times
in his letters); and of St John's writings (Gospel and
three Epistles) 'eternal life'. It is true that the person of
Jesus Christ is bound up, in one way or another, with
all three themes. But how? Have we not, in fact, here
three messages or 'Gospels' instead of one?

A little knowledge of the New Testament (as Bacon
would say) may incline a man to this view; but a deeper
study will bring his mind round to a conviction of its
essential unity. For when, with the aid of modern
scholarship, we study these three themes just mentioned,

we begin to see that when Jesus said: 'The Reign of God has come' (the implication being, in His person and ministry) and Paul: 'If any man be in Christ, he is a new creature' (or perhaps, better, with the RV Mg., 'there is a new creation'); and John: 'The Word became flesh and dwelt among us', they were not making different and unrelated statements; on the contrary, they were using different idioms and thought-forms to express their common conviction that with the coming of Christ the living God had spoken and acted decisively for the salvation of His people. Further, we begin to see that, in spiritual terms, 'to be in the Kingdom of God' is not really different from what Paul calls 'being in Christ' and John describes as 'having eternal life'.

In short, beneath the obvious diversity of the New Testament there is a deep and fundamental unity of message: a unity that must have been felt (if not clearly discerned) by the men who gathered the twenty-seven books together to form a Canon. A musical metaphor will perhaps make the point clearer: If there are in the New Testament many musicians (at least a dozen) playing different instruments, one dominant theme sounds through all their music. What is that theme, and how shall we entitle it?

In one phrase, it is 'The Story of Salvation'—the story of how in the fullness of time God completed His saving purpose for His People by sending His Son, the Messiah, and of the means of salvation. On this summary of the New Testament message some elucidatory comments are necessary.

To begin with, the message of the New Testament is, at bottom, precisely what we have called it—a *story*. It is the story of how God decisively intervened in human history in the person of Jesus Christ. It is a story in a form so simple that children can grasp it, though its profound implications for man and the world and history must be worked out by theologians. It is a story that for its expression needs the use of active verbs, such as 'God spoke' or 'sent' or 'gave'. It is a story that finds its classic expression in John 3.16, 'God so loved the world that he gave his only begotten son that whosoever believeth on him should not perish, but have eternal life.'

Next, notice that this story is the completion of God's saving purpose for His People. This again is a point of capital importance. We cannot understand the New Testament aright unless we see it against a background of the Old, unless we see the story of the New Testament as the completion of the story which begins *in* the Old. Myers has put the whole matter in a verse:

'God who to glean the vineyard of His choosing
    Sent them evangelists till day was done,
Bore with the churls, their wrath and their refusing,
    Gave at the last the glory of His Son.'

'In brief, it is the same God who speaks to us in both the Old and the New Testaments'; as it is 'one purpose of God which is being fulfilled throughout both, one People of God the story of which is being told from Abel to the Apostolic age'. This point finds its classic expression in Hebrews: 'God having of old time spoken unto the fathers in the prophets by divers portions and in divers manners, hath at the end of these days spoken unto us in his Son' (Hebrews 1.1 f.).

Finally, notice that this story of salvation, though one and indivisible, can be resolved into three elements: A

Saviour, a saved (and saving) People, and the work of salvation itself. These are three strands in a single cord —a trinity in unity—and that unity is the story of salvation.

Now if there were space, it would be possible to show at length that this triune story (if the phrase will be allowed) runs through the whole New Testament. But we must content ourselves with a brief summary now.

First, then, through the New Testament there runs what we have called the *kerygma*, that is, the message of salvation which centres in Jesus Christ, the Saviour. Mark, the earliest Gospel, is simply an expanded form of this *kerygma*; and so, with some differences, are the other three Gospels. All four (as Professor Dodd has shown) are '*kerygma*-built'. This same message is the staple of the apostles' preaching as we find it in Acts. It is the underlying presupposition of all Paul's theology and thinking, peeping out from time to time as in I Cor. 15.3 ff. And it is the basis too of the writings of the apostolic men from Hebrews to Revelation. And the burden of this message or *kerygma* is simply this: As the scriptures had foretold, in the life, death, resurrection, and exaltation of Jesus the Messiah and in the outpouring of the Spirit, God has come into our world in His kingdom, power and glory (though the glory, as John says, is a death upon a cross) for us men and for our salvation.

But a Saviour implies a saved People. And the second strand in the unity of the New Testament message is its doctrine of the Church as the new and true People of God. (The roots of this doctrine go back of course into the Old Testament, where Israel, or the faithful remnant, is conceived of as the People of God.) Through the whole New Testament runs this doctrine of the People of God, called into new being by God through Christ, and appointed to spread abroad in the world the Good News of salvation.

First, we see Jesus in the Gospels dedicating Himself to His God-appointed task of gathering God's People. He calls twelve disciples (the People of God in miniature) whom He instructs in the principles of the Kingdom, before sending them forth on a mission to gather the faithful. But He also sees clearly that the task to which He has been called can only be completed by the death and resurrection of the Shepherd of the 'little flock' (as He names the embryo Church). He dies, and rises, and on the day of Pentecost the new People of God, now empowered by the Spirit, begins a new and glorious chapter in its history, of which the end is not yet. So, in Acts, as the Gospel is carried from Jerusalem to Rome, we see the People of God, called the *Ecclesia* or Church, grow into a great multitude. And this same conception of the Church as the People of God, owning its sole allegiance to Christ its head and filled with the Spirit, informs and permeates the Epistles of St Paul and the writings of the other apostolic men down to the Book of Revelation.

Thirdly and lastly, we find that the story of salvation in its third aspect, or element, runs right through the New Testament. That third element is the saving work of Christ—what we usually call the atonement. Not Jesus only but Paul and all the apostolic men assert that the root-cause of man's malaise and misery in this world is sin, which breaks the fellowship with God for which man is designed; as they, one and all, assert that in Christ and especially through His sacrificial death on the Cross, the barrier between God and man has been done away and a new way of access to God been opened up for sinful men. In fine, 'through the New Testament there runs one mighty thought: Christ died for our sins: He bore what we should have borne; He did for us what we could never have done for ourselves: He did for God that which was God's good pleasure.'[1]

Here then, in barest summary, is the triune story of salvation of which the New Testament is the record. This is the 'Word from the Beyond for our human predicament' which gives the New Testament a place apart in the religious literature of the world. And this story of salvation is the basis of all sound Christian doctrine to-day, the inspiration of all true Christian living, and the foundation on which rests any true Christian belief in the life everlasting.[2]

[1] J. K. Mozley, *The Doctrine of the Atonement*, p. 93.
[2] For a detailed exposition of the unity of the New Testament along these lines see the present writer's book with this title (published by the S C M Press).

BIBLIOGRAPHY

TRANSLATIONS

A New Translation of the New Testament: JAMES MOFFATT.
The Revised Standard Version.

INTRODUCTIONS

The best short and up-to-date book is *An Introduction to
the New Testament* by F. B. CLOGG. Though not an introduction in the strict sense of the word, *The Riddle of the
New Testament* by HOSKYNS and DAVEY will introduce the
reader to the main New Testament issues. The present
writer's *Interpreting the New Testament* summarizes the
story of New Testament scholarship in the last fifty years.

LANGUAGE

On the Language see B. M. METZGER'S article in *The Interpreter's Bible*, Vol. VII, 43–59.

TEXT AND CANON

On the Text we recommend SIR F. G. KENYON: *The Story
of the Bible*, and on the Canon, HARNACK'S *The Origin of
the New Testament*.

BACKGROUND

A. C. DEANE: *The World Christ Knew.* For the Jewish
side, the student should read EDWYN BEVAN'S article on
'Environment' in GORE'S one-volume *New Commentary
on Holy Scripture*; the Greek side is brilliantly sketched in
T. R. GLOVER'S *The Conflict of Religions.* If the student
finds G. A. SMITH'S *Historical Geography of the Holy Land*
too big for his purpose, he will get instruction as well as
pleasure from H. V. MORTON'S two books *In the Steps of
the Master* and *In the Steps of St Paul.* Two other useful
books are *The Westminster Historical Atlas to the Bible*
and (for archæology) JACK FINEGAN'S *Light from the
Ancient Past.*

THE THEOLOGY OF THE NEW TESTAMENT

JAMES DENNEY: *Jesus and the Gospel* (an old but very valuable book); A. E. J. RAWLINSON: *The New Testament Doctrine of the Christ*; C. H. DODD: *The Apostolic Preaching and its Developments*; H. A. A. KENNEDY: *The Theology of the Epistles*; A. M. HUNTER: *Introducing New Testament Theology*.

THE FOUR GOSPELS

On the Synoptic problem the student should begin with B. H. STREETER'S fine article in PEAKE'S one-volume *Commentary on the Bible*; go on from that to V. TAYLOR'S *The Gospels* (where he will also learn something about Form-criticism); and if he wish more, to STREETER'S monumental *The Four Gospels*.

For a commentary on the teaching of Jesus there is nothing better in English than *The Sayings of Jesus* by T. W. MANSON. C. H. DODD'S *Parables of the Kingdom* is a new and delightful window on an old landscape. The *Parables of Jesus* by JOACHIM JEREMIAS is an attempt to recover the original form and meaning of the Gospel parables. The problem of miracle is well handled in D. S. CAIRNS'S *The Faith that Rebels*, and ALAN RICHARDSON'S *The Miracle Stories of the Gospels*.

On the life of Jesus we suggest GORE: *Jesus of Nazareth*; T. R. GLOVER: *The Jesus of History*; H. E. W. TURNER: *Jesus Master and Lord*. The present writer's *The Work and Words of Jesus* attempts to provide a modern sketch of the subject.

On the Fourth Gospel W. TEMPLE'S *Readings in St John's Gospel* is admirable for the general reader. Johannine theology is ably summarized in W. F. HOWARD'S *Christianity according to St John*.

ACTS AND ST PAUL

Along with a good commentary on Acts, e.g. that by Blunt in the Clarendon Bible Series, the student should read SIR WILLIAM RAMSAY'S *St Paul the Traveller and Roman Citizen*.

If he find PATERSON SMYTH'S *Life and Letters of St Paul* too elementary, he will find *St Paul* by A. D. NOCK a *multum in parvo*. Paul's theology is ably expounded in J. S. STEWART'S *A Man in Christ* or C. H. DODD'S *The Meaning of Paul for To-day*. The present writer's *Interpreting Paul's Gospel* may be found helpful. Finally, he should not miss DEAN INGE'S splendid essay on the man Paul in *Outspoken Essays* (*First Series*).

THE WRITINGS OF THE OTHER APOSTOLIC MEN

Here we pick out four books: ROBERT LAW'S *The Tests of Life* (a brilliantly written exposition of First John); E. F. SCOTT'S *The Book of Revelation* (a lucid introduction to a mystifying book); C. E. B. CRANFIELD'S *The First Epistle of Peter*; WILLIAM MANSON'S *The Epistle to the Hebrews*.

COMMENTARIES ON THE NEW TESTAMENT

One-volume Commentaries on the Bible include: *Commentary on the Bible*, edited by A. S. PEAKE; *A New Commentary on Holy Scripture*, edited by CHARLES GORE; *The Abingdon Bible Commentary* (an American production) and (much simpler) *The Teacher's Commentary* (completely revised), edited by G. HENTON DAVIES and ALAN RICHARDSON and published by the SCM Press.

Then there are several series of commentaries on the New Testament. We name only these on the English text: (1) *The Westminster Commentaries*; (2) *The Century Bible*; (3) *The Clarendon Bible*; (4) *The Moffatt New Testament Commentary* (based on DR MOFFATT'S Translation) now complete; (5) *The Torch Bible Commentaries* (SCM Press), and (6) *The Interpreter's Bible*, both in process of appearance.

One word more to the student. Do not expect too much from commentaries. Commentaries are often incredibly dull and useless affairs, as inspired commentators are few and far between. A good commentary can indeed help to clear our text for us and by illuminating details enhance our enjoyment of the sacred author. But a bad commentary by piling up 'accidents and irrelevancies' can hide the fair face of the text from us. Therefore let the student weigh well the word of Bengel, one of the very greatest of our commentators:

> 'Te totum applica ad textum:
> Rem totam applica ad te.'

or as we might translate it:

> 'To give thyself unstinted to the text aspire:
> Then to thyself apply its point entire.'

INDEXES

(a) SUBJECTS

'Access', 162 f.
Acts of the Apostles, 70–78
Advent, Second, 184 f.
Apocalyptic, 186–188
Apollos, 97, 157 f.
Aramaic, 17
Autographs, 19 f.

Babylon, 170, 189
Bishops, 149, 181
Blackstone, Henry, 54

Canon, 22–25
Cerinthus, 175
Christ, the Cosmic, 134 f., 138
Church, as Body of Christ, 102, 127
Churches, the Seven, 188 f.
Colossae, 134, 143
Colossians, Epistle to the, 134–138, 145
Colossians and Ephesians, 120 f.
Corinth, 97
Corinthians
  First Epistle to, 97–104
  Second Epistle to, 105–111
Cursives, 21

Decree, Apostolic, 84, 114
Delphi, inscription at, 86, 140
Diotrephes, 180 f.
Disciple, the Beloved, 61 f.
Diversity of N.T., 195 f.
Docetism, 175, 179
Domitian, 189

Enoch, Book of, 182
Ephesian Ministry, Paul's, 89 f.
Ephesians
  Epistle to, 120–127
    Authorship of, 120–122

Faith and works, 118, 165 ff.
Felix and Festus, 88
Freedom, Christian, 112, 119

'Galatia', problem of, 112–114
Galatians, Epistle to, 112–119
Gamaliel, 80
Gnosticism, 134, 149
Gospel, meaning of word, 29
Greek, classical and common, 17–19

Hebrews, Epistle to the, 157–163
Hope, Christian, 168, 194, 200
Hymns, 125, 153

Incarnation, doctrine of, 15, 177 ff.

James, Epistle of, 164–167
James, the Lord's brother, 164
John, Gospel according to, 61–69
John, Epistles of, 174–181
John, the Apostle, 61 ff.
John, the Elder, 63, chapter XXV *passim*

John, the Seer, 188
Joy, Christian, 133
Judaizers, 114 f.
Jude, Epistle of, 182 f.

Kerygma, 29 f., 198

Language of N.T., 17–19
Life, eternal, 64, 174 ff., 195
Logia, 37
Longinus and Procula, 78
Love, Christian, 69, 178, 180
Luke, Gospel according to, 48–54
Luke, the Evangelist, 48 ff., 71 ff.

'Man of sin', 141
Mark, Gospel according to, 32 f., 40–47
Mark, John, 32 f., 41 f., 83
Marriage, problems of, 60, 100
Matthew, Gospel according to, 55–60
Matthew, the Apostle, 37
Muratorian Canon, 24

Nero, 40, 169, 192
Niemöller, 128

Onesimus, 120, 143–147
Origen, 157

Papias, 37, 41
Papyrus, 19 f., 61
Paraclete, the, 68
Pastoral Epistles, 148–156
  Authorship of, 148–150
Paul, Life and letters of, 79–90
Peter
  First Epistle of, 168–173
  Second Epistle of, 184 f.

Philemon, Epistle to, 143–147
Philippi, 128 f.
Philippians, Epistle to, 89 f., 128–133
Plerōma, 136
Proto-Luke, 51

Quelle, 35 f., 38
Quotations, Patristic, 21

Resurrection, 102 f.
Revelation, Book of, 186–194
Romans, Epistle to, 91–96

Salonica, 139
Salvation, 196 ff.
'Severe Letter' to Corinth, 106 f.
Signs, 65 f.
Silvanus, 168–170
Stephen, 81, 161
Synoptic Problem, 34–39

Tarsus, 79
'Tests of Life', 176 f.
Text of N.T., 19–22
'Thankful Letter' to Corinth, 106 f.
Theophilus, 51, 71
Thessalonians, Epistles to, 139–142
Timothy
  First Epistle to, 150–152
  Second Epistle to, 152–154
Titus, Epistle to, 154 f.
Tradition, oral, 29–32, 34

Uncials, 21
Unity of N.T., 195–200

Versions of N.T., 21

'We passages', 49, 85
Word, Jesus as the, 65

(b) AUTHORS

Anton, 148
Augustine, 10

Barth, 14
Bengel, 75, 133, 204
Bevan, 201
Browning, 66 f., 70, 138, 178

Cairns, 202
Calvin, 96, 120
Carlyle, 143, 178
Clogg, 60, 201
Coleridge, 96, 120
Cranfield, 203

Dale, 29
Deane, 54, 201
Deissmann, 71
Denney, 48, 155, 202
Dodd, 40, 46, 93, 120, 126,
    198, 202, 203
Duncan, 87

Findlay, J. A., 77, 165
Finegan, 201

Glover, 9, 201, 202
Goethe, 15
Goodspeed, 120
Gore, 203

Hanson, 105
Harnack, 12, 53, 201
Harrison, 150
Hoskyns, 68
Hoskyns and Davey, 201
Howard, 69, 202

Inge, 81, 203

Jeremias, 202

Kennedy, H. A. A., 202
Kenyon, 201
Klausner, 11

Law, 176, 203
Levertoff and Goudge, 59
Luther, 79, 96, 112, 147, 164

Mackay, 120
Macneile, 169
Manson, T. W., 25, 36, 202
Manson, W., 161 f., 203
Masefield, 78
Metzger, 201
Meynell, 134
Moffatt, 50, 92, 145, 170, 201,
    203
Morton, 201
Mozley, 200
Myers, 197

Neil, 142
Niebuhr, 180
Niemöller, 128
Nock, 203

Peake, 203

Ramsay, W. M., 76, 85, 113,
    202
Rawlinson, 202
Renan, 48
Richardson, 202, 203
Robertson, J. A., 176

Scott, C. A., 93
Scott, E. F., 193, 203

Scott, Sir Walter, 68
Sheppard, 12
Smith, G. A., 201
Smith, W. R., 16
Smyth, Paterson, 203
Stevenson, 168
Stewart, 203
Streeter, 38, 42, 57, 62, 179, 181, 182, 202

Taylor, 32, 202
Temple, 62, 202
Tennyson, 65
Turner, 202

Von Hügel, 133

Westcott and Hort, 22
Wordsworth, 68